JOSEPH
AND
MORONI

Joseph Smith Jr.

JOSEPH
AND
MORONI

THE 7 PRINCIPLES
MORONI TAUGHT
JOSEPH SMITH

LEGRAND L. BAKER

EBORN BOOKS

2007

This book is the opinion of the author
and does not represent the official views of
The Church of Jesus Christ of Latter-day Saints.

First Edition, First Printing

Library of Congress Control Number: 2006929938
ISBN: 1-890718-99-8

Eborn Books
Salt Lake City, Utah
ebornbk@doitnow.com
www.ebornbooks.com

Printed in the United States of America

To the Memory of
Dr. Robert Andrew
1934 - 1984
of
Madison, Wisconsin

TABLE OF CONTENTS

List of Illustrations by Jared Merrill

Jared Merrill was born in Provo, Utah in 1987. He graduated from Woods Cross High School in 2005. There, he was chosen Student Body Artist, and the Art Sterling Scholar. He has completed one year at Brigham Young University, and is currently serving an L.D.S. mission.

ACKNOWLEDGMENTS

It began more than thirty years ago, just after I received a Ph.D. from the University of Wisconsin at Madison, and just before my family moved to Arkansas where I had a teaching position. Two of our dearest friends, Robert and Emy Andrew, invited my wife and I, and our children to share a few days of their vacation with them and their children on Strawberry Island, in the finger of Lake Michigan near Green Bay, Wisconsin. When Sunday evening came, Robert asked me to tell the children a story about Joseph Smith. I told them about Joseph and Moroni. The amazing thing was that they all listened—they didn't wiggle and they didn't fall asleep—and because they were listening, the story lasted much longer than any of us expected. Robert and Emy later urged me to write the story as I had told it.

We remained in Arkansas for two years before we came to BYU. During our stay in Arkansas, I wrote this history of the friendship between Joseph and Moroni. My wife Marilyn read and proofread it; then we sent it to Robert and Emy who polished its language to make it more appropriate for teenagers. Several drafts passed back and forth this way.

Over the years at BYU, I added chapters and changed it to fit the interests and language of my friends who were students at the university. I asked some of them to have a go at making it sound more sophisticated and grown up. Then, after I retired, I met Bret Eborn who published my book, *The Murder of the Mormon Prophet*. I told Bret about this manuscript and he asked to see it. That presented a major challenge! Before I could give it to him, I had to take out some, but not all, of the things my friends and I had added, and put the manuscript back into its original language.

Besides my wife Marilyn, Robert and Emy, Bret Eborn, and Beverly Campbell (who wrote the introduction), there are many other friends to whom I am grateful for their interest in this little history. I thank them for their friendship as much as for their interest, and for helping to keep the story alive. I also thank Jared Merrill, who drew the illustrations.

Most of all, I thank the children—my children and the Andrew children—who were the inspiration that caused me to write the story, and whom I love very much.

LeGrand Baker
Orem, Utah

INTRODUCTION BY BEVERLY CAMPBELL

LeGrand Baker has been my friend and associate for more than 20 years. I am constantly astounded at his abilities—and through this book I think you will find a joy in a journey that will please and enlighten you.

This is a story about a boy and the angel who taught him how to be a prophet—but it is not a story just for boys, it is for everyone, male, female—young, old. As Joseph's epic journey comes to life in these pages, narrated by a great story teller and a careful researcher into truth, one is moved, informed, instructed and enlightened. There is no one in the church who should not know this story in all its nuances and who would not benefit from a careful reading of this book. For those not of our faith, it provides exceptional insight into the workings of a loving and benevolent God.

Importantly, this is our story—our reality—our truth. It brings to light, with amazing clarity and urgency, facts not commonly known and presents significant and important new insights. It focuses on seven principles that Moroni taught Joseph. These principles are fundamental to the spiritual well-being of every Latter-day Saint

Certainly Joseph's life, the authority and revelations he received, and the courageous and heroic acts he performed are the most important of this the Last Dispensation before the second coming of our Savior.

At a very personal level, one finds in Joseph's story a mirror into one's own grand journey, which helps enormously as we seek to make sense of all that life demands of us. In these pages you become acquainted, in a most personal way, with struggle—an intense and sometimes disappointing struggle—as Joseph tries to live to the standard that would mold him into the individual that

God needs him to be to complete his foreordained mission. As you are further drawn into Joseph's training in heavenly counsels, and learn of his assignments you are led to a clearer understanding of your own pre-mortal training and are caused to ponder what it is that you might have agreed and committed to. Watching Joseph being prepared, step by necessary step, one realizes more fully that each of us also made covenants which we do not now remember but which the Holy Ghost will teach us how to fulfill as we struggle in this world.

True to the story as Joseph lived it, the book carries with it the implicit understanding that none of this is designed to be easy, and that there always will be mistakes, but if one listens to the Spirit and lets the Lord use one's mistakes to teach and inform us, the ultimate reward is spiritual success.

Central to this epic is the relationship of a great general, historian, messenger, envoy and herald of God with our young Joseph. You follow their relationship grow into trust and friendship as the maturing, learning, growing, sometimes stumbling Joseph, becomes a man worthy to become the Prophet.

In exploring this grand and unique relationship, between General Moroni and Joseph we learn that Moroni not only devoted the last years of his own life to compiling that record which Joseph was to locate and translate—but that he needed to hide it where Joseph could find it some years later. Additionally Moroni needed to watch over it until it was Joseph's turn on earth, and throughout its retrieval and translation. Such a combining of missions does cause one to ponder about the time Joseph and Moroni surely spent together in a pre-mortal realm as their plans were laid. What does this teach us about our own relationships with God and our other fellow travelers?

You come to know Joseph's parents, his brothers, the challenges they faced as a family and individually. You come to understand the concept of angels as you understand that Joseph was ministered to by not just one but many angels. You learn that over a period of time he became as at home in the presence of these angels as in the presence of his earthly family and friends. The angels were his friends, his teachers, his mentors and in certain instances his chastisers and disciplinarians. In so doing we better understand the role such beings can and should play in our own lives.

Reading this book you also learn of the nature and reality of two other great—but competing forces in your life—Satan, the destroyer, and the Holy Ghost, the grand restorer, the one who protects and brings light into your life. You learn about friends and enemies, about betrayers and those you can trust. You learn about loving and being led to that person you can love. You learn about being given gifts and losing gifts, about being broken hearted and about being healed. You learn of things sacred and those who would wish to profane them. You learn about the true nature of God and what it means to live to have His countenance in your face.

Beverly Brough Campbell has had a long and distinguished career as a mother; as a driving force behind many national and international public and private educational and philanthropic projects. During the critical Cold War Years, and immediately prior to and after the collapse of Communism in Eastern Europe she was Director of International Affairs of The Church of Jesus Christ of Latter-day Saints.

While living in the Washington, D. C. area, she served as the Coordinating Director of the Joseph P. Kennedy Foundation. In addition to their work with the mentally handicapped, she also helped set up and administer grants establishing bio-ethical studies at major universities. She played a defining role in the creation and administration of Special Olympics.

During the twelve years she was Director of International Affairs for The Church of Jesus Christ of Latter-day Saints, she served as a resource to the Council of the Twelve Apostles. She initiated and maintained positive working relationships with congressmen, ambassadors, and world leaders, not only in the nation's capital, but also at the U.N. and in national capitals throughout Europe, Asia, Africa, and other nations and islands of the seas, as needed. Before the collapse of the Berlin Wall she was in contact with the Ministers of Religion in the governments of most of the Iron Curtain countries. Through exhaustive diplomatic efforts her office was able to open doors which allowed the first L.D.S. missionaries into many of these countries, establish ties with new governments and enhance opportunities to participate in establishing religious liberty laws.

In civic affairs her contributions have ranged from assisting Mrs. Liana Dubinin, wife of the former Soviet Ambassador, in establishing Children of Crisis (an organization which now serves throughout Europe); to serving on the board of directors of Utah Festival Opera. She is a member of the President's Roundtable of Advisors and School of Management's National Advisory Committee at Brigham Young University. She is a founding member of the American Family Society and has worked with many other private foundations and groups at a national and international level addressing such diverse challenges as child survival, breast cancer, drunk driving, media, and interfaith cooperation. Her private family international interests include providing fresh water wells, text books, and assisting in the building of concrete dams for villages in Africa. In 1998 Brigham Young University awarded her the prestigious Presidential Medallion.

An in-demand speaker, she is also the author of several articles and two best selling books: *Eve and the Choice Made in Eden* and *Eve and the Mortal Journey: Finding Wholeness, Happiness, and Strength.*

She and her husband, A. Pierce Campbell, are the parents of three children, and the grandparents of six.

JOSEPH SMITH AND MORONI

This is the true story of how an angel taught a boy to be a prophet. As a testimony of Joseph Smith, the story is important. But it is important for reasons that reach far beyond that. Moses once observed, "Would God that all the Lord's people were prophets, and that the Lord would put his spirit upon them!" (Numbers 11:29) Moses did not say, "Would God that all the Lord's priesthood holders should be prophets"; he said, "that all the Lord's people."

That has always been the desire of the Lord's servants. It was the overshadowing intent of all that Joseph sought to accomplish. It is not about everyone's seeking to become the President of the Church. That is a special kind of prophet with specific priesthood authority. It is about what Moses said: "that the Lord would put his spirit upon them" that every person in the church could conduct his or her life according to one's personal revelations from heaven.

The object of this little book is to examine the principles taught by Moroni to Joseph. Moroni's task was to teach Joseph how to become the prophet he was foreordained to be. The book addresses the question, "What must one do to be that kind of prophet?" The principles are as universal as they are eternal. They are as applicable to girls as to boys—and they are as applicable to every man and every woman as they were then applicable to the young Prophet Joseph.

As any great teacher would, Moroni used Joseph's experiences to teach him those principles. The seven principles Moroni taught Joseph are as follows:

First principle: one does not speak too openly
about sacred things

Second principle: one must learn how to recognize
the feeling that identifies the Holy Ghost

Third principle: integrity is
keeping one's covenants with God

Fourth principle: sometimes prophets
must make their own decisions

Fifth principle: friendships, however important,
are not as important as keeping
God's commandments

Sixth principle: the Lord has already planned
for his children's success

Seventh principle: the Lord provides whatever help
he understands we need.

First Principle:
One Does Not Speak Too Openly about Sacred Things

An Extraordinary Friendship

Joseph Smith's relationship with Moroni was not that of a docile young man and an angel without a personality. Moroni was a prophet and a general who had watched his people destroy themselves because they would not obey the Lord. Joseph was an intelligent, strong-willed teenager who liked to do things his way. So there were times when there were conflicts.

It might have been easier if the angel had "broken" and trained Joseph the way one might break and train a spirited young horse. But if Joseph were to be trusted with the powers of priesthood, he must also be trusted to exercise those powers in the full strength of his own personality. A prophet obeys God. If he does not obey, he is not a prophet; but if he is not free to disobey, he is only a puppet. A prophet and a puppet are not the same thing. A prophet obeys because he chooses to obey.

Joseph would be successful only to the degree that the enormous potential he brought with him into this world was allowed to fully develop.[1] Joseph had to be taught to be obedient without taking away his sense of individual worth, without warping his strong personality, and without violating the law of his own being. In short, he was to be taught how to obey, but he was not to be "broken."

The extraordinary friendship that developed between the angel and the boy was molded by their mutual respect, and then forged and tempered by Joseph's need to keep his balance—to not be overwhelmed by it all. On the one hand, Joseph walked with angels and knew their purposes; on the other, he was only a boy struggling to become a man. Moroni was patient but would not be diverted from his objectives: to prepare Joseph to receive the plates of the Book of Mormon, to teach him how to translate them, and ultimately to teach him how to be a prophet. The angel's studied patience suggests he was working on this principle: just as one can not be tempted beyond one's ability to withstand,[2] so it is true that one can not be given spiritual experiences and insights more quickly than one is willing and able to assimilate them.[3]

THE FIRST VISION

Joseph was no weakling. He was a tall, athletic, self-assured, good-looking lad who enjoyed physical labor and vigorous play. He worked on his father's farm and earned some money by "hiring himself out" to work for neighbors. One of those neighbors was Martin Harris, a well-to-do farmer who recalled that after hoeing corn all day, Joseph liked to relax by wrestling. Martin's report that he and

Joseph liked to relax by wrestling

Joseph often wrestled with each other shows that there was a pleasant and easy friendship between them.[4]

Joseph had very little formal schooling, but his learning was adequate for the time. His father had been a school teacher,[5] and the family frequently read together. The Bible was the best-selling book on the New England frontier, and the Smiths, like their neighbors, read the Bible. Joseph did not read as much as other members of his family; he spent more time thinking—"given to meditation and deep study" is the way his mother described him.[6]

Joseph was only fourteen years old when he became the focal point of one of the most important events of human history. There are four versions of his First Vision that can be attributed directly to him. The most important is the one in the Pearl of Great Price, but the others are interesting also. The following are excerpts from all four of them:

> 16. But, exerting all my powers to call upon God to deliver me out of the power of this enemy which had seized upon me, and at the very moment when I was ready to sink into despair and abandon myself to destruction—not to an imaginary ruin, but to the power of some actual being from the unseen world, who had such marvelous power as I had never before felt in any being—just at this moment of great alarm, I saw a pillar of light exactly over my head, above the brightness of the sun, which descended gradually until it fell upon me.
>
> 17. It no sooner appeared than I found myself delivered from the enemy which held me bound. When the light rested upon me I saw two Personages, whose

brightness and glory defy all description, standing above me in the air. One of them spake unto me, calling me by name and said, pointing to the other—*This is My Beloved Son. Hear Him!*

18. My object in going to inquire of the Lord was to know which of all the sects was right, that I might know which to join. No sooner, therefore, did I get possession of myself, so as to be able to speak, than I asked the Personages who stood above me in the light, which of all the sects was right (for at this time it had never entered into my heart that all were wrong)—and which I should join.

19. I was answered that I must join none of them, for they were all wrong; and the Personage who addressed me said that all their creeds were an abomination in his sight; that those professors were all corrupt; that: "they draw near to me with their lips, but their hearts are far from me, they teach for doctrines the commandments of men, having a form of godliness, but they deny the power thereof."

20. He again forbade me to join with any of them; and many other things did he say unto me, which I cannot write at this time. (J.S.-History:16-20a).[7]

Another version reads:

I retired to a secret place in a grove and began to call upon the Lord while fervently engaged in supplication my mind was taken away from the objects with which I was surrounded, and I was enwrapped in a heavenly vision and saw two glorious personages who exactly resembled each other in features, and likeness, surrounded with a brilliant light which eclipsed the sun at noon-day.[8]

A third version reads:

A pillar of light above the brightness of the sun at noon day came down from above and rested upon me and I was filled with the spirit of God; and the Lord opened the heavens upon me and I saw the Lord and he spake unto me saying, "Joseph, my son, thy sins are forgiven thee. Go thy way, walk in my statutes, and keep my commandments. Behold I am the Lord of Glory. I was crucified for the world that all those who believe on my name may have eternal life. Behold the world lieth in sin at this time, and none doeth good, no not one. They have turned aside from the gospel and keep not my commandments. They draw near to me with their lips while their hearts are far from me; and mine anger is kindling against the inhabitants of the earth to visit them according to this ungodliness, and to bring to pass that which hath been spoken by the mouth of the prophets and Apostles. Behold and lo, I come quickly, as it is written of me, in the cloud, clothed in the glory of my Father. And my soul was filled with love, and for many days I could rejoice with great joy, and the Lord was with me but I could find none that would believe the heavenly vision.[9]

The final version reads:

> Information was what I most desired at this time, and with a fixed determination to obtain it, I called on the Lord for the first time in the place above stated, or in other words, I made a fruitless attempt to pray. My tongue seemed to be swollen in my mouth, so that I could not utter. I heard a noise behind me like some one walking towards me. I strove again to pray, but could not; the noise of walking seemed to draw nearer. I sprang upon my feet and looked around, but saw no person, or thing that was calculated to produce the noise of walking. I kneeled again, my mouth was opened and my tongue loosed; I called on the Lord in mighty prayer. A pillar of fire appeared above my head; which presently rested down upon me, and filled me with unspeakable joy. A personage appeared in the midst of this pillar of flame, which was spread all around and yet nothing consumed. Another personage soon appeared like unto the first: he said unto me, "Thy sins are forgiven thee." He testified also unto me that Jesus Christ is the son of God. I saw many angels in this vision. I was about 14 years old when I received this first communication.[10]

While Joseph's accounts of the First Vision redefine the traditional Christian concept of God, he actually wrote very little about what he saw or about what he was told. One cannot know the full story of the First Vision because Joseph chose not to tell it. His accounts contain enough detail that one may know the events immediately preceding it and know its conclusion—that no church had the true gospel and that it would be Joseph's responsibility "to bring to pass that which hath been spoken by the mouth of the prophets and Apostles." However, concerning the particulars of the vision itself, Joseph preserved a reverent silence.

There are many accounts in the scriptures of visions in which prophets of old were told about their own foreordinations and calls to serve. In some accounts the prophets mention angels gathered in a heavenly temple, singing praises to their God.[11] Joseph's "I saw many angels" may be a reference to that kind of experience.

One wonders how much like the visions recorded by the ancient prophets Joseph's might have been, and a comparison is interesting. It would be a mistake to try to superimpose their accounts of their visions on young Joseph's First Vision. However, the following comparison is relevant, if to do nothing more than teach about the modest and unpretentious personality of Joseph Smith.

Joseph wrote, "I saw a pillar of light exactly over my head, above the brightness of the sun, which descended gradually until it fell upon me." Through Joseph's words one senses an encompassing serenity in that hovering, blazing pillar. But for Ezekiel, it was like a tornado: "I looked, and, behold, a whirlwind came out of the north, a great cloud, and a fire infolding itself, and a brightness was about it, and out of the midst thereof as the colour of amber, out of the midst of the fire."[12]

Joseph did not share Ezekiel's need to express the dramatic; it was more in keeping with his personality (and perhaps with his culture) to content himself with just being sure that his record was correct and understandable. On another occasion the young prophet described a "cloud of light" in connection with the visit of John the Baptist, again conveying a sense of peace more than of wonder. For him, all that needed to be said was that, "a messenger from heaven descended in a cloud of light."[13]

Joseph's account of his First Vision never takes his readers from the rural setting in which he was most comfortable, and that homespun elegance never loses its sense of reverence. "I was enwrapped in a heavenly vision,"[14] and "when the light rested upon me I saw two Personages, whose brightness and glory defy all description, standing above me in the air."[15] Isaiah, on the other hand, transports one to the heavenly temple where he "saw also the Lord sitting upon a throne, high and lifted up, and his train filled the temple."[16] Lehi not only told his family about God's throne, but also about the angels who were there: "He was carried away in a vision, even that he saw the heavens open, and he thought he saw God sitting upon his throne, surrounded with numberless concourses of angels in the attitude of singing and praising their God."[17]

There are other characteristics that appear in many, but not all, of the accounts of a prophet's call.[18] Like Lehi's, the call often takes place during a meeting. The location, when specified, is in the throne room of the Celestial Temple. Members of the Council in Heaven are in attendance, singing hymns of joy to God. At these meetings several things occur: (*a*) Earth life and the plan of salvation are discussed. (*b*) There is a vote taken or a covenant made by which those present express their assent to the proposed plan. *(c)* Specific assignments, in terms of earth-times, places, and objectives, are made to individual prophets and to those who are foreordained to assist them. (*d*) In conjunction with those assignments, ordinances[19] and ordinations[20] are performed.

In these visions the prophets see their own foreordinations. They are shown that in the heavenly councils they were given assignments that included the authority to speak for God.

When the prophets describe these foreordinations to their readers, they use different symbols. For Jeremiah, that moment was when the Lord put forth his hand and touched Jeremiah's mouth, saying: "I have put my words in thy mouth. See, I have this day set thee over the nations."[21] John the Beloved describes his receiving the authority to speak for God by writing that he was given a little book to eat. That book was symbolic of both his foreordination and his mission.[22] Lehi also was given a book, but he was asked to read it. In it he learned of the destruction of Jerusalem and of his responsibility to warn the people.[23] For Isaiah that symbol was a burning light. One of the seraphim took a live coal from the altar of the temple and placed it on Isaiah's lips to purge his iniquity, apparently giving him authority and power to speak the Lord's words to Israel.[24]

Ezekiel spends about a page explaining the responsibilities of the call he received at that time. Nephi takes a little less space to tell about his father's call. Jeremiah uses 19 chapters to describe his and alludes to it often thereafter.

The candor of Isaiah's reaction to his call is delightful. Isaiah was shown a meeting in the temple in the premortal existence. In the vision, probably while watching himself participate in a discussion about a dangerous situation that was going to develop on the earth in about 750 B.C., he heard, as he had heard aeons before, "the voice of the Lord, saying, Whom shall I send, and who will go for us?" Isaiah saw his own response: "Here am I; send me." The Lord reviewed what Isaiah's assignment would be. After a little consideration on Isaiah's part, that assignment looked a bit heavy, and he asked, "Lord, how long?" The Lord gave a straight-forward, but not very comforting, reply: "Until the cities be wasted without inhabitant, and the houses without man, and the land be utterly desolate."[25] "Oh. I just thought I would ask," one can almost hear Isaiah sigh to himself.

There is nothing like that in Joseph's story. For him it was sufficient to report that he was told not to join any church and then to add, with a note of solemn self-understanding, "and many other things did he say unto me, which I cannot write at this time."[26]

JOSEPH LEARNS NOT TO TALK TOO OPENLY ABOUT SACRED THINGS

When young Joseph left the grove that day, he must have felt as though all the world lay at his feet. One can feel the memory of his self-assurance in his own report of the conversation between him and his mother. He wrote: "As I

"Never mind, all is well—"

leaned up to the fireplace, mother inquired what the matter was. I replied, 'Never mind, all is well—I am well enough off.'"

Almost anyone who has ever reared a fourteen-year-old boy need only look to the surface of one's own imagination to discover the twinkle in Joseph's eye, the suggestive rise of the eyebrow, and the knowing smile when he added, "I have learned for myself that Presbyterianism is not true." (J.S.-History 1:20).

Joseph's account of his own response to his First Vision brings one quickly back to the realization that, notwithstanding the vision's magnitude and overwhelming importance, its recipient was still a boy—a vulnerable, tender, young boy.

After the First Vision, his "soul was filled with love,"[27] and he soon interpreted that feeling as a need to tell others what had happened. But he was surprised and disappointed to discover that many of his friends reacted by mocking him rather than believing his story:

> I soon found, however, that my telling the story had excited a great deal of prejudice against me...and was the cause of great persecution.... I was led to say in my heart: Why persecute me for telling the truth? (J.S.-History 1:21-25).

In his enthusiasm to share the great truths he had learned, Joseph was introduced to an eternal principle, that he, like most of us, had to learn the hard way:

The cost of knowing is that one does not tell unless the Spirit says to tell. It is beyond the scope of human ability to teach the mysteries of godliness. Only the Spirit can do that. If our words will help, we are instructed to talk; otherwise we violate a sacred trust when we impose unwanted truth upon those who are not prepared to listen. One does not trifle with sacred things and discuss them as interesting bits for idle conversation. Alma explained that even though it is given to many to know the mysteries of God, those many do not have license to tell whomever they choose. Implicitly, if we insist on talking out of turn and persist in doing so, our hearts will be hardened to the sacredness of the truth. When that happens, we abdicate our right to know, and then we forget. Alma says that not knowing the mysteries of God is called "the chains of hell." (Alma 12:9-11).

Well before he met Moroni, Joseph learned, by unhappy experience, this most important lesson: Telling about a sacred experience must be as precious as having the experience; otherwise one does not tell at all. Moroni would re-enforce that principle when he explained that Joseph must show the plates to no one until he had permission to do so.

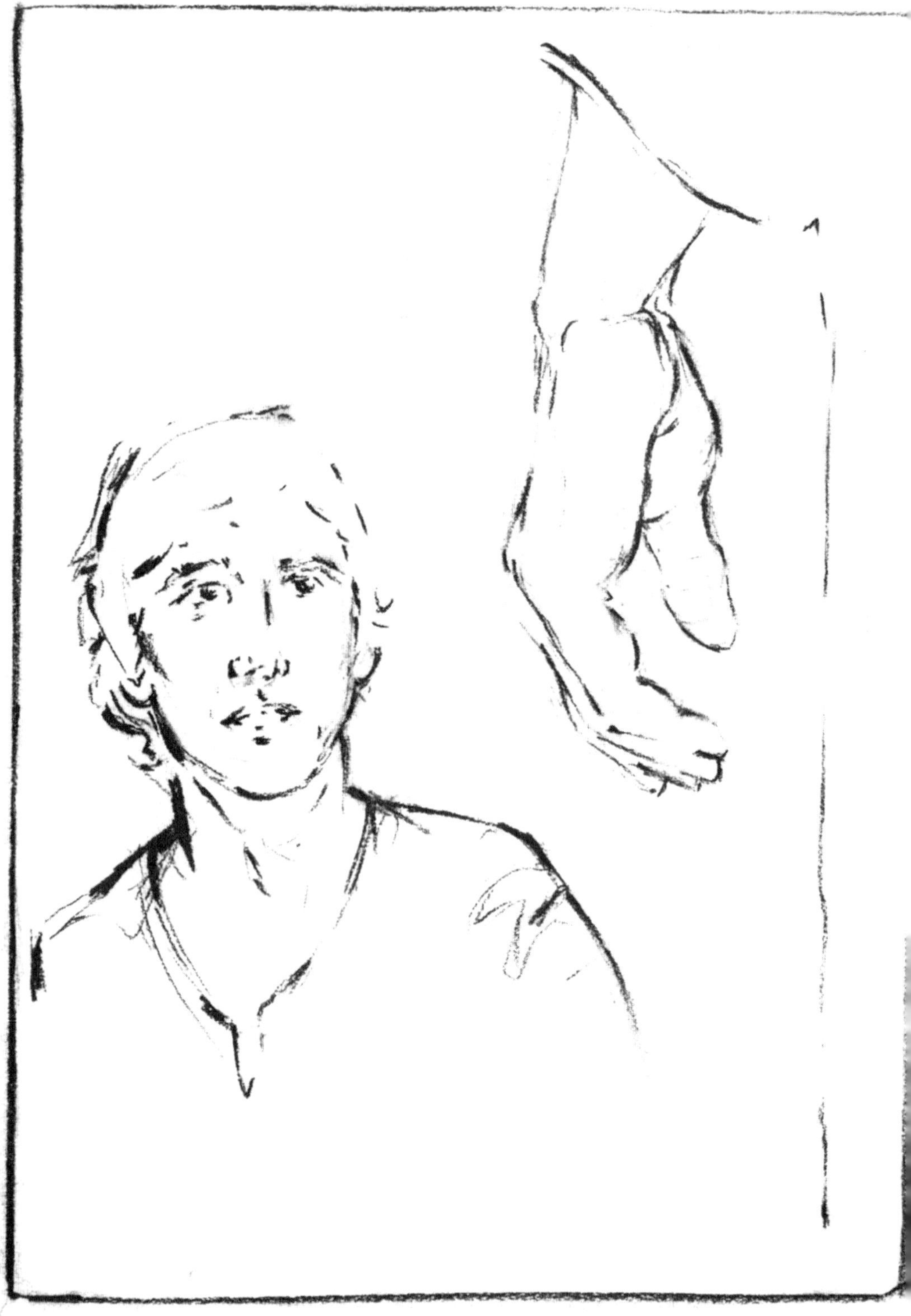

SECOND PRINCIPLE:
ONE MUST LEARN HOW TO RECOGNIZE THE FEELING THAT IDENTIFIES THE HOLY GHOST

JOSEPH MEETS MORONI

Joseph was eighteen years old when he met Moroni. It was a Sunday evening in September 1823, four years after the First Vision. Perhaps inadvertently, Joseph told a great deal about those four years when he recorded that on that Sunday evening he began his prayer with "full confidence in obtaining a divine manifestation." (J.S.-History 1:29).

Whatever else he had done in those years, he had been preparing himself, and he now felt ready for additional instruction from the heavens. And—and this is important —it was he who, responding to the Spirit, recognized that he was ready, and it was he who asked. Asking questions —especially when the Spirit suggests the questions—is a necessary prelude to knowing the answers.

The rest of the family had already gone to bed when Joseph knelt to pray. As he prayed, he noticed the darkness of his room gradually displaced by a light that grew brighter and brighter until his little room was "lighter than at noonday." Within the light he saw an angel standing in the air beside his bed.

> [The angel wore] a loose robe of most exquisite whiteness. It was a whiteness beyond anything earthly I had ever seen.... Not only was his robe exceedingly white, but his whole person was glorious beyond description, and his countenance truly like lightning." (J.S.-History 1:30-32).

That was a more dramatic answer to Joseph's prayer than he had expected—or else it was just that there was something really awesome about the angel. Joseph's first reaction was to be afraid. But when Moroni spoke, Joseph's fear went away and their friendship began. (J.S.-History 1:32).

WHO WAS MORONI?

We need to stop here, freeze time at the moment of Moroni's smile and ask ourselves: "Who were these two men whose lives were separated by about 1,400 years, but whose missions were so tightly interwoven by the responsibilities the Lord had given them? How much did they know about each other?"

Part of that second question can be handled very readily. Because Joseph chose to tell very little about the First Vision and almost nothing about what had occurred to make him confident that he would receive an answer when he knelt to pray that night, one does not know whether Joseph knew anything at all about Moroni. But the other part of that question, "How much did Moroni know about Joseph?" has a very different answer.

Since before his own death, more than 1400 years earlier, Moroni had read the record that identified Joseph by name,[28] and had looked forward to this time when they could work together.

As a young man, Moroni may have spent much of his time watching or even helping his father, Mormon, prepare the Book of Mormon. When Moroni wrote the conclusion of the Book of Mormon, he had been so aware of the person who would eventually translate his writings that he actually wrote a short note to him. Moroni was then abridging the book of Ether and had just finished explaining that the brother of Jared had seen a vision of the whole history of the world. (Ether 3:26). To that explanation he added, "I have written upon these plates the very things which the brother of Jared saw;" (Ether 4:4). then, Moroni penned this note to the future prophet:

> 1 And now I, Moroni, have written the words which were commanded me, according to my memory; and I have told you the things which I have sealed up; therefore touch them not in order that ye may translate; for that thing is forbidden you, except by and by it shall be wisdom in God.
>
> 2 And behold, ye may be privileged that ye may show the plates unto those who shall assist to bring forth this work;
>
> 3 And unto three shall they be shown by the power of God; wherefore they shall know of a surety that these things are true.

> 4 And in the mouth of three witnesses shall these things be established; and the testimony of three, and this work, in the which shall be shown forth the power of God and also his word, of which the Father, and the Son, and the Holy Ghost bear record—and all this shall stand as a testimony against the world at the last day. (Ether 5:1-4).

Moroni had devoted the last part of his own life to completing the book and hiding it where Joseph could find it. After his death, Moroni remained responsible for the plates, waiting for the time when he could turn them over to young Joseph.

Moroni obviously knew the scriptures about Joseph's mission; he quoted many of them to Joseph during their interview that night. The Book of Mormon itself contains several. Among them are rather general ones that tell about the last days; more specific ones that tell about the coming together of the scriptures of Joseph and Judah and the story of Martin Harris going to Professor Anthon; and very specific ones which deal with Joseph himself: "Behold, I will reveal unto you the Priesthood, by the hand of Elijah the prophet, before the coming of the great and dreadful day of the Lord." (J.S.-History 1:38).

Moroni would have known all of that about the young prophet, but it seems likely that he knew much, much more. It seems to me that in the spirit world they would have discussed their missions at great length.[29] The difference now was that Moroni could remember those conversations and Joseph could not.

So when one considers what Moroni must have known, one also wonders what he must have felt and what he was thinking as he stood there, looking down at that eighteen-year-old boy who was kneeling beside his bed, full of wonder—a little bit afraid—and trying to discover if the angel was friendly.

MORONI'S MESSAGE TO JOSEPH

Moroni introduced himself and told the young man that God had a work for him to do. The beginnings of that work would focus on ancient records written on plates of gold. They contained the fullness of the gospel of Jesus Christ and were buried in a hill near Joseph's home. Joseph would also find the Urim and Thummim which would help the young and untrained prophet translate the Book of Mormon and receive and understand revelations from God.

Moroni then recited a number of prophecies from the Bible that foretold Joseph's work in restoring the gospel, gathering Israel, and establishing the latter-day kingdom of God. Some of these scriptures Joseph identified in his history. Others he concealed behind these words: "He quoted many other passages of scripture, and offered many explanations which cannot be mentioned here."[30]

After reciting the scriptures, and apparently while speaking within the context of their explanation, Moroni gave Joseph a stern warning. Joseph recalled, "He told me;... I should not show them to any person...only to those to whom I should be commanded to show them; if I did I should be destroyed."[31]

While Moroni was telling Joseph about the plates, he showed him where they were hidden. Joseph saw in vision the Hill Cumorah and the place near its top where he would find a box made of stone and cement. Its lid was a rounded stone, shaped like a turtle shell and partly exposed above the ground. The treasures were in the box.

After the angel had delivered his message, the light gathered around him. Then Joseph saw "a conduit open right up into heaven." The angel ascended through that conduit of light until he passed from view. The room was then as dark as it had been before.

Joseph lay there thinking about his visitor and what the angel had said, when his room began to fill with light again. Moroni returned and reviewed everything he had told Joseph.

This time when the angel left, Joseph was wide awake. As he lay there thinking, his room filled with light a third time. Moroni appeared and repeated it all again, adding this warning: Satan was aware of the importance of Joseph's mission and would try to divert him by calling his attention to the worth of the gold. Therefore, the angel commanded, Joseph was not even to think about using the plates to get rich.[32]

As Moroni left the third time, the rooster crowed. That primitive but effectual alarm clock told Joseph that the three visitations from Moroni had lasted the entire night—suggesting that each visit lasted longer than two hours. One

"Why did you not tell your father?"

could learn a lot from an angel in two hours. With the Holy Ghost to drive home his message, and with visions (like showing Joseph the box on the hill) as the ultimate visual aids, Moroni must have flooded Joseph's mind with new ideas.

One marvels at the intellect of that young man. The fact that he could assimilate so much new information so quickly, speaks of a quality of genius that leaves one in dizzied admiration.

Moroni's Fourth Visit

Joseph joined his family for breakfast as usual that morning. Then he, his father, and the rest of the older boys went out into the field to work. As the morning passed, Joseph's father noticed that his son seemed tired and weak, and he suggested that Joseph go back to the house to rest. This might have been Joseph's cue, but even though he remembered Moroni's parting instructions "to tell his father all which he had both seen and heard,"[33] he left the field without saying anything about it.

He got as far as the fence, tried to climb over it, lost his strength altogether, and fell to the ground. He lay there, under the shade of an apple tree, until he was aroused by Moroni's voice.[34]

"Why did you not tell your father?" the angel wanted to know.

Joseph replied that he was afraid his father would not believe him.

"He will believe every word you say to him," was the angel's response. Then, for the fourth time, Moroni repeated everything he had told Joseph the night before, including the vision and the warning. He told the boy to go back to the field where his father was and to tell him what he should have told him already.[35] This time Joseph obeyed.

When his story was finished, Joseph Smith Sr. told his son that "it was of God," and urged him to go to the hill where the plates were hidden and do whatever else the angel instructed him to do.[36]

Joseph left the field again. This time he went directly toward the Hill Cumorah. Oliver Cowdery later wrote the story as Joseph told it to him. Joseph said that as he walked, he began to think about the plates, but more especially about the gold.[37] When he got nearer the hill, "it seemed as though two invisible powers" were contending with each other to see which could "influence his mind." When he arrived at his destination, his struggle abated—but not in victory, for Joseph had lost the battle: when he found the half-buried box, he had "a fixed determination to obtain [the gold] and aggrandize himself."[38] He had decided to sell the plates.

JOSEPH FINDS THE PLATES

Joseph easily recognized the large, turtle-shaped stone concealing the golden treasure. He moved the soil from

using a lever, he lifted the lid

around its edges; then, using a lever, he lifted the lid and saw the gleaming book.[39] Its pages measured about eight by ten inches and were about as thick as "common tin." Ancient Egyptian-like writing had been engraved into each page, evincing the skill of the prophets who had cut the words into the metal. The pages were bound together by three gold rings, making a volume about six inches thick. Part was sealed, and Joseph would never be permitted to open those pages.[40] Beside the plates in the box lay an ancient ceremonial sword. Its blade was made of the "most precious steel"; its hilt was "pure gold."[41] Beside that lay the Urim and Thummim, which appeared to be two large diamonds set in a rim of silver bows and fastened to a breastplate.[42]

Joseph looked for a moment and then reached down to pick up the book of gold. When his hands touched it, he received a severe shock. Surprised and weakened, he tried again. Again he was shocked and rendered weaker than before. He decided this must be some device used by the angel to protect the plates; but then Joseph was strong and able, and just now he was very determined. He seized upon the plates with all his strength. This time the shock was so severe that he was hurled backward onto the ground. He lay there, stunned, but more puzzled than injured.

"Why can I not obtain this book?" he wondered aloud, even though he saw no one who might answer him.

"Because you have not kept the commandments of the Lord."[43] Moroni was standing there, looking down at him—still talking about obedience.

A clear recollection of the angel's warnings came rushing in upon Joseph's consciousness as he realized that he had done something terribly wrong.

> At that instant he looked to the Lord in prayer, and as he prayed darkness began to disperse from his mind and his soul was lit up as it was the evening before, and he was filled with the Holy Spirit; and again did the Lord manifest his condescension and mercy: the heavens were opened and the glory of the Lord shone round about and rested upon him.[44]

"Look," the angel commanded. Joseph saw a vision of himself, as he had walked toward the hill only a few minutes before. He watched as "the prince of darkness, surrounded by his innumerable train of associates," accompanied Joseph along the road and up the hill. The devil had spoken to his consciousness, and what had seemed to Joseph to be only the wanderings of his mind began to focus on the gold and then on the money it might bring. After seeing that vision, Joseph understood how the promised glitter of the gold had come to outshine his memory of the glory of the angel. Moroni explained,

> All this is shown, the good and the evil, the holy and impure, the glory of God and the power of darkness, that you may know hereafter the two powers and never be influenced or overcome by that wicked one.[45]

MORONI SHOWS JOSEPH THE DIFFERENCE BETWEEN GOOD AND EVIL

Moroni insisted that Joseph must never forget the difference between the feelings associated with the prompting of the devil and the feelings associated with the prompting of the Holy Ghost. He said that Satan "fills the hearts of men with evil," and teaches them "to walk in darkness." Moroni also explained, "the way of holiness is peace and rest."[46]

The contrast was clear. There are three sources of the thoughts that seem to just pop into one's head. The first is simply one's Self. Some thoughts may be memories or a conglomerate of the things one has seen or read or experienced. The mind has the incredible ability to remember such things almost at will and sometimes to gather them in fresh bouquets and arrange them into what seem to be wholly new ideas. These sudden insights are often called "inspiration." The feeling of exhilaration when that happens is something that has to be experienced, for it cannot be described, but it is wonderful.

The second source of one's ideas is the devil. Those insidious notions are not so wonderful. They leave one frightened or angry or ill at ease—or prompt the more dangerous feelings of greed, thirst for power, or the need to get even. While these may come from one's own mind, they may also be, like Joseph's desire for gold, ideas planted by the devil. If so, one can always identify them by the dark feelings that accompany them.

The third source of ideas is the Holy Ghost. The feeling that identifies the Holy Ghost is like a harmony of one's most cherished senses of well-being: love, peace, and security all blended as one. Yet it is different from any of those. It "tastes" differently from the others—just as the taste of an orange is different from the taste of a strawberry or an apple. If one were asked to describe the tastes of those fruits, one would use the same words to describe each: "sweet, perhaps a bit tangy, very good." The words do not describe the differences: one must taste the fruits to know they differ from one another. But after one has tasted them, one can easily tell them apart. The feeling that is associated with the Holy Ghost is like that. With a little practice, one can easily recognize it and can distinguish it from any emotional feeling one might have—and fortunately, there is a way to practice. The Holy Ghost testifies that the Book of Mormon is true, so one of the very best ways to practice identifying it, is to read the Book of Mormon, pray, and pay very close attention to one's feelings as one is taught the truth of individual passages and ideas in the scripture.

The Holy Ghost is important for at least four reasons:

(1) He can be trusted all the time, whereas one's emotions cannot.

(2) Because he can be trusted, his influence and the information he gives increases one's options, and therefore enhances one's agency.

(3) He heightens one's ability to experience joy.

(4) He makes repentance effective, and cleanses one from the effects of sin. These do not happen all at once, but

they develop slowly, with faith, repentance, prayer, and practice.

These ideas are so important that they need to be discussed in some detail.

First: The Holy Ghost can be trusted all the time, whereas one's emotions cannot.

Because the feeling that identifies the Holy Ghost can not be self-initiated—like happiness or excitement can be when one reads a good book or sees a movie—it cannot be counterfeited by one's own enthusiasm or sincere desire. But we can mis-identify those emotions for the Holy Ghost if we do not know what He feels like. For example, if we want something very badly, pray earnestly to have it, and in our enthusiasm are sure that God shares our desires, we may become convinced the Holy Ghost has answered, "Yes." Then, when one does not get it, one might say, "But I prayed, and I felt good about it." Just feeling good about something is not the same as receiving a revelation. However, when we learn to identify the feeling that is always associated with the Holy Ghost, we also learn to trust that feeling. Then the Holy Ghost becomes a source of strength, as well as of inspiration.

Before Joseph could be secure in his calling as a prophet—one who speaks in behalf of God—he had to learn to sort his ideas by recognizing their sources. He had to know by his feelings, and through his own experiences, whether an idea (or an emotion like joy, reticence, or fear) was the product of his own mind or a suggestion from the devil or an instruction from the Lord. Until he could know that—unerringly, by being able to identify the feeling that comes from the Holy Ghost—he could not trust his own sense of revelation. Indeed, until he could make those distinctions with absolute certainty he would not really be free to know or to choose.

Second: Because the Holy Ghost can be trusted, his influence and the information he gives increases options, and enhances agency.

Freedom to choose can be a reality only when we can distinguish between our choices. If we do not know the source of our ideas, then we cannot know which idea we can trust, because unless we know the source of the ideas from which we may choose, we cannot accurately predict the consequences. If we do not know the consequences, then we are able to exercise no more real freedom of choice than one who is asked to choose when he has been blindfolded. Freedom to guess and freedom to choose are not the same thing. Freedom to guess is being given the right to choose while being denied the criteria upon which one may judge. That is only pretended freedom. It may look like freedom—we may even accept it as freedom—but in reality it is a kind of slavery instead. The inspiration from the Holy Ghost actually gives us freedom to choose. In asserting this, we must acknowledge that the temporary blessings of the Holy Ghost and the permanent gift of the Holy Ghost are not the same thing, but they are of the same source. Thus, the testimony that comes to a new convert before baptism is as valid and as consistent with truth as the personal revelations received after baptism.

Third: The Holy Ghost heightens one's ability to experience joy.

Parley P. Pratt described this better than anyone else ever has:

> The gift of the Holy Spirit adapts itself to all these organs or attributes. It quickens all the intellectual faculties, increases, enlarges, expands and purifies all the natural passions and affections; and adapts them, by the gift of wisdom, to their lawful use. It inspires, develops, cultivates and matures all the fine-toned sympathies, joys, tastes, kindred feelings and affections of our nature. It inspires virtue, kindness, goodness, tenderness, gentleness and charity. It develops of person, form and features. It tends to health, vigor, animation and social feeling. It develops and invigorates all the faculties of the physical and intellectual man. It strengthens, invigorates, and gives tone to the nerves. In short, it is, as it were, marrow to the bone, joy to the heart, light to the eyes, music to the ears, and life to the whole being.[47]

Fourth: The Holy Ghost makes repentance effective, and cleanses one from the effects of sin. These do not happen all at once, but they develop slowly, with faith, repentance, prayer, and practice.

In the Book of Mormon, Moroni explained:

> And after they had been received unto baptism, and were wrought upon and cleansed by the power of the Holy Ghost, they were numbered among the people of the church of Christ. (Moroni 6:4).

The cleansing does not happen all at once. It comes slowly, in stages, as one repents. In each stage, the other effects of the Holy Ghost are increased, until, as Moroni wrote,

> And again, if ye by the grace of God are perfect in Christ, and deny not his power, then are ye sanctified in Christ by the grace of God, through the shedding of the blood of Christ, which is in the covenant of the Father unto the remission of your sins, that ye become holy, without spot. (Moroni 10:33).

The lesson Joseph learned from that experience on the hill that day was prerequisite to his obtaining the plates—and to his becoming secure in his calling as a prophet. Only after he could, with absolute certainty, recognize different sources of his feelings, could he know when he was speaking and acting as a prophet of God; and only then could God trust him to be His Prophet. Moroni explained to him:

> You have now beheld the power of God manifested and the power of Satan: you see that there is nothing that is desirable in the works of darkness; that they cannot bring happiness; that those who are overcome therewith are miserable, while on the other hand the righteous are blessed with a place in the kingdom of God where joy unspeakable surrounds them.[48]

Moroni cautioned that even though Joseph would learn to distinguish between the promptings of the Holy Ghost and those of Satan, this alone would not altogether remove the young prophet from the reach of the devil. The angel warned that notwithstanding Joseph had seen this great display of power, by which he might "ever be able to detect the evil one," the fact that Joseph knew how to recognize and cope with Satan would not diminish the adversary's ability to use other people as a tool by which he might hurt the young prophet. Moroni warned:

> When it is known that the Lord has shown you these things, the workers of iniquity will seek your overthrow: they will circulate falsehoods to destroy your reputation, and also will seek to take your life; but remember this, if you are faithful, and shall hereafter continue to keep the commandments of the Lord, you shall be preserved to bring these things forth; for in due time he will again give you a commandment to come and take them....
>
> You now see why you could not obtain this record; that the commandment was strict, and that if ever these sacred things are obtained they must be by prayer and faithfulness in obeying the Lord.[49]

That was why Moroni kept talking about obedience!

Before Joseph left the hill, Moroni cautioned him once more: this would not be Satan's last attempt to overwhelm the young prophet. "Forget not to pray, that thy mind may become strong, that when he shall manifest unto thee, thou mayest have power to escape the evil, and obtain these most precious things."[50] Buried in that promise was a loving, fearful warning: there would be a time "when he shall manifest unto thee."

In his first attempt to receive the plates of the Book of Mormon, Joseph was introduced to what would probably be the most important lesson of his life: his power as a prophet lay in his will to obey. Only he himself could choose how he would respond to his diverse feelings. He must be able to recognize their sources in order to choose intelligently and confidently between them.

A prophet must be a person of unbending integrity. But such a quality has little virtue if there is a gap between what is truth and what the prophet perceives to be truth. So, first of all, a prophet must be one who can know, through his own cognizance, that his own ideas, attitudes, and actions square with eternal truth. Then he must have the integrity to *be* what he *knows*. [51]

It may be that the kind of perfection to which each Latter-day Saint aspires will remain out of reach until one can identify with equal certainty the sources of the ideas that seem to just pop into one's head. The enticements of Satan are utterly ineffectual as a weapon against any righteous person who can identify the source of an idea and who, through that identification, is free to choose whether he will act upon the idea or spurn it.

Before Joseph left the hill, Moroni explained to him that:

> the time for bringing them [the plates] forth had not yet arrived...but he told me that I should come to that place precisely in one year from that time, and that he would there meet with me, and that I should continue to do so until the time should come for obtaining the plates. [52]

"And that I should continue to do so until..." implies that Joseph understood that there would be lessons that he could not learn in just one year. Indeed, it would take four years before Joseph was ready.

Even though Moroni told Joseph he must leave the plates in their box, the young prophet felt secure in what he had learned. Many years later, Joseph's mother remembered:

> While Joseph remained here, the angel showed him, by contrast, the difference between good and evil, and likewise the consequences of both obedience and disobedience to the commandments of God, in such a striking manner, that the impression was always vivid in his memory until the very end of his days; and in giving a relation of this circumstance, not long prior to his death, he remarked, that ever afterwards he was willing to keep the commandments of God.[53]

THIRD PRINCIPLE: INTEGRITY IS KEEPING ONE'S COVENANTS WITH GOD

JOSEPH TEACHES HIS FAMILY ABOUT THE PEOPLE OF THE BOOK OF MORMON

The evening after that first interview with Moroni, Joseph waited until after supper, and then told the story to his whole family.[54]

"From this time forth," his mother recalled, "Joseph continued to receive instructions from the Lord."[55] As time passed, Moroni not only told Joseph about the contents of the Book of Mormon, but showed him, in vision, the peoples and, events about which the book was written. In doing this, Moroni used the best possible method of preparing Joseph to participate in the work of translation. One who understands a people, their culture, their history, and the impact of their ideas upon events is far better able to translate their writings correctly than one who only has an academic background in their language.

Moroni began to teach Joseph about the Book of Mormon four full years before Joseph had the plates. There are no firsthand accounts of these visions, but in the evenings, after the day's work was done, the Smith family would gather around, "all seated in a circle...and giving the most profound attention," while Joseph taught them."

Occasionally during these evening conversations, Joseph told them about the culture of the people whose history was in the book that still lay buried in the box on the hill. His mother wrote:

> He would describe the ancient inhabitants of this continent, their dress, mode of traveling, and the animals upon which they rode; their cities, their buildings, with every particular; their mode of warfare; and also their religious worship. This he would do with as much ease, seemingly, as if he had spent his whole life among them.[56]

For Joseph to have known the ancient Americans that well, his tutorials with Moroni must have been as vivid as movements through time.

JOSEPH GOES TO THE HILL CUMORAH THE SECOND TIME

On the twenty-second of the next September, exactly one year after the day he first climbed the hill to see the plates, Joseph was to return to that same place. Because of his frequent contact with Moroni, visits from the angel must have long since ceased being a novelty to the young prophet. But if Moroni thought of them as routine, he certainly had not stopped taking them seriously. In preparation for Joseph's second attempt to get the plates, Moroni cautioned Joseph that he must beware of other people's greed. Some would try to steal the plates to get the gold. If they were stolen and melted down, the words, which were more precious than the gold, would be lost. To emphasize the danger and to clarify Joseph's responsibility, Moroni told him that once the plates were in Joseph's custody, he must not lay them down or let them out of his hands for even a moment, until they were safely hidden. Joseph promised he would obey.

Oliver Cowdery tells us that on the appointed day, Joseph climbed the hill to the place where the stone box was buried, opened it, reached in, picked up the plates, and started back down the hill. Then he stopped, remembering he had not replaced the stone lid on the box. The sword and other treasures were still exposed to the view of anyone who might pass by, and he realized they might be stolen. He returned, laid the plates down beside him where they would be safe, and pushed the heavy lid back into place. When the box was closed, he turned to pick up the plates. They were gone! Joseph could not understand what had happened. He had heard no one approach, yet someone had taken them. He was frightened and terribly frustrated when he knelt to ask the Lord for help.

As had happened a year before, Moroni responded to Joseph's pleadings. And, as before, Joseph's ex-general, angel tutor told him he could not have the plates until he had learned to obey. Moroni's insistence that Joseph promise to keep the plates safe and not let them out of his hands should have been taken more seriously. That golden record had been prepared as the key of the restoration of the gospel, of

He returned, laid the plates down...

the restoration of Israel, and of the fulfillment of the covenants that the Father had made in the beginning. The plates were precious beyond price and needed to be protected with the utmost care. Since Joseph could not yet be trusted to look after them, Moroni had returned the plates to their box.

Moroni gave Joseph permission to look. Once again the young man pried open the lid. When he saw the plates, he reached down to take them in his hands, "but instead of getting them, as he anticipated, he was hurled back upon the ground with great violence."[57]

He just lay there. Now the angel was gone, the box was closed, and Joseph was alone. He had been weighed in the balance of his own integrity, and found wanting. When he recovered his strength, he returned to his parents' home, weeping with grief and disappointment.[58] One can almost hear the echo of the angel's instructions in young Joseph's sobbing: "*You must learn to obey*!"

ANOTHER LESSON ABOUT OBEDIENCE

The plates were the angel's responsibility. He could protect them well enough when they were in his custody, and he would not let Joseph have them until Joseph had learned to follow his instructions explicitly. Joseph had chosen to not obey, so now he must wait another year.

Stories like this ask questions, and one of the most intriguing is, "Why?" Moroni was able to move the plates—there can be no doubt about that. Why then did he not just pick them up and take them down to the house and give them to Joseph? Why must Joseph come to their hiding place to get them? Why must he come year after year? Those questions all suggest the same answer: There were things Joseph needed to learn that only time and experience could teach him.

When Joseph first climbed that hill to get the plates, he understood that his folks were very poor. Loving sons are conscious of those things, and his history records his memory of it. He wrote,

> As my father's worldly circumstances were very limited, we were under the necessity of laboring with our hands, hiring out by day's work and otherwise, as we could get opportunity.[59]

Perhaps the notion of selling the gold began there. It is not a bad thing for a young son to wish he could help his parents. The beginning of his temptation may only have been something like this: "I wonder if there might be just one page at the back that does not have writing on it, and I could sell that one to help my dad." An idea like that could have been the entree for the rest. Deceit then followed deception until the devil had manipulated Joseph's thinking.

That conjecture on my part might or might not account for Joseph's first failure to get the plates. Still, after he had once succumbed to the enticements, he ought to have recognized and avoided them. Indeed, he did. There is no evidence that Joseph ever again entertained the notion of selling the gold.

Joseph's second attempt to get the plates was altogether different from the first. He was foiled, not because he wanted to sell the treasure, but because he wanted to protect it. This time Joseph may have thought, "After all, the angel does expect me to be responsible. Would a responsible person walk away, leaving a silver bow and breastplate and a priceless sword lying there in the open to be stolen by whoever might pass by? If I were responsible I would have closed that lid." Convinced by his own reasoning, Joseph returned. But since he could not move the heavy stone with the plates in his hands, he had to lay them down.

So, one might ask, what was there about those two experiences that was a necessary element in the maturation of this young prophet? What did he learn?

In both of those possible scenarios, Joseph's temptation was not to do something bad, but to do what Joseph himself understood to be best. The sin was that he did not do what the Lord told him would be best. The lesson he learned was that when a prophet acts in behalf of the Lord, he does what the Lord tells him to do.

Integrity means that there is no gap between what one says and what one does. Integrity is a personal power that is either the key to our salvation or the surest way to go to hell. If we love the Lord and his children, and act in accordance to that love, and under the direction of the Holy Ghost, then integrity has become the key to salvation. However, if we support some unholy cause, then personal integrity—the persistence in following that unrighteous path—will prevent us from acknowledging the truth and, therefore, from repenting.

Joseph's returning to close the box was an expression of his own integrity. That would have been a good thing under any other circumstances, but this time his integrity should have caused him to do what he was told to do—to hold tightly to the plates until they were properly hidden.

The lesson he learned was this: just as a prophet must be able to tell the difference between ideas that come from the devil and those that come from the Lord; so a prophet must also be able to tell the difference between the ideas that come from the Lord and those that come from his own mind. If Joseph had not learned that principle, he could not have been a prophet.

FOURTH PRINCIPLE: SOMETIMES PROPHETS MUST MAKE THEIR OWN DECISIONS

JOSEPH GOES TO THE HILL THE THIRD TIME

Moroni told Joseph that he could not embark on this great adventure alone—that when he came to receive the plates from the angel, he must bring someone with him.

"Who?" Joseph asked.

"Alvin, your oldest brother."[60]

Alvin had been a strength to the young prophet from the first. If there was anyone in this world Joseph could trust it was Alvin. Notwithstanding that trust, Joseph could not tell anyone everything.

The things Joseph knew must have imposed a dreadful loneliness upon the young man. He needed someone who could believe what he said and not demand that he say too much—someone who would accept and love him as a person and not expect that he always act the part of the Elijah-bringing-down-the-fire prophet and sage. There were many things Joseph could not tell; it was as though he were required to walk alone. Moroni had been alone,[61] and he apparently understood how important it was that Joseph have someone who would walk beside him—even in his aloneness. It must have been a great comfort for Joseph to know there would be someone else he could depend on and trust and that the angel would approve of such a relationship.

But Alvin died, and his death left a dreadful void in Joseph's life. When Joseph climbed the hill to see Moroni he really was alone, and the angel would not let him have the plates. Joseph Knight, one of the young prophet's most trusted friends, tells the story:

> [When Alvin died, Joseph] did not know what to do. But when the 22nd day of September came, he went to the place [where the book was buried] and the personage appeared and told him he could not have it now. But the 22nd day of September next he might have the Book if he brought with him the right person.[62]

Joseph was no longer a teenager, and it was time for him to find a wife. She must be worthy and willing to come with him to the hill when he received the plates. She must be as noble as he; and it was necessary that he find her and marry her before, not after, he was entrusted with the plates.

Joseph asked the angel, "Who is the right person?"

Moroni replied, "You will know."[63]

A Prophet Is Not a Puppet

When one sees the years in which Joseph tried to receive the plates as a single experience, one discovers the formula that may be called "How a boy may become a prophet"—not "How to become President of the Church," because that is a unique kind of prophet; but how to become a prophet in one's own life—to ourselves, our families, and in whatever else the Lord asks us to do.

Joseph had learned the first three principles—and they are much simpler to say than to do.

First, learn to tell the difference between the feeling that comes with the Holy Ghost and the temptations from the devil.

Second, learn to tell the difference between the prompting of the Holy Ghost and one's own desires, whether they come in the form of emotions, enthusiasm, fear, wanting to go with the crowd, or even sometimes one's sense of what is okay. That second principle is more difficult than the first, because it seems to strike at the very essence of one's Self. But if one can learn to do that, then one becomes free to follow the Spirit.

Third, in Moroni's words to Joseph, "You will know," God expects one to make intelligent, well informed decisions. If those decisions are incorrect, then the Holy Ghost will sound a warning, but prophets do not just sit and do nothing until they get instructions.[64] The whole purpose of the first two rules is to teach one correct principles so one can make intelligent decisions until one's own sense of right and wrong is consistent with what God understands is good and bad. Moroni taught Joseph to be a prophet, not a puppet. A prophet and a puppet are not the same thing. When our sense of right and wrong is correct and imbedded into our personality, the consequence is happiness and security in our relationship with God. A major purpose of the Holy Ghost is to facilitate an understanding of one's Self by one's Self, so that within the full scope of one's own strengths, one can make and act on correct decisions—knowing always, that the Holy Ghost will sound a warning if the decisions are not correct.

When Joseph began to look for a wife, he had a great advantage. If Joseph Knight is correct in his account, the young prophet looked into the Urim and Thummim to find out where to find Emma. That he did so is evidence that he had access to the Urim and Thummim and had learned how to use them a long time before he got the plates.[65] That he selected his wife-to-be that way is evidence that he trusted the Lord. That he loved her and she him is evidence that the Lord loved and understood them both.

JOSEPH'S FINAL PREPARATIONS TO RECEIVE THE PLATES

On January 18, 1827, Joseph married Emma Hale and brought her to Palmyra to live in his parents' home. Moroni, like a good friend, had apparently kept out of the way while Joseph and Emma were falling in love and beginning their life together. But, also like a good friend, he understood what to do when the time came to bring Joseph's attention back to his mission. The angel chose to do that on an evening when Joseph was alone, walking along the quiet country road near the Hill Cumorah.

Joseph Married Emma Hale

Joseph had set off early that morning to do an errand for his father and was returning about suppertime. As he passed the hill where the plates were buried, the angel was waiting for him. They talked together for about three hours that night. Moroni chastened Joseph because he "had not been engaged enough in the work of the Lord." Joseph said Moroni told him that "the time had come for the record to be brought forth; and that I must be up and doing and set myself about the things which God had commanded me to do."[66] Moroni also told Joseph that "he should make another effort to obtain the plates, on the twenty-second of the following September."[67]

What else was said during those three hours Joseph does not say, but that conversation made a deep impression on the young prophet. He described it to his parents as "the severest chastisement that I have ever had in my life." Yet in that same conversation he confidently reassured his father, "Give yourself no uneasiness concerning the reprimand which I have received, for I now know the course that I am to pursue, so all will be well."[68] Those words (as his mother records them) are a key to young Joseph's personality. Now that he knew what to do, he would do it; since he would do it, all would be well. One sees great strength hidden amid the unpretentious strains of that declaration, for, indeed, that is the ultimate declaration of one's own independence. For this young prophet "knowing what to do" and "all will be well" were equivalents.

After that long visit with Moroni, Joseph resolved to "be up and doing."

> From this time forward he continued to receive instructions concerning the coming forth of the fulness of the gospel, from the mouth of the heavenly messenger, until he was directed to visit again the place where the record was deposited.[69]

As before, there was a condition—the one Moroni had written in the book itself.[70] Joseph must not show the plates to anyone until the translation was completed and Joseph was ready to return them to the angel's custody. When that time came, Moroni promised, Joseph would be permitted to show the plates to a few people whom the Lord should designate. Joseph promised. This time, notwithstanding being subjected to a great deal of pressure to break that promise, Joseph obeyed. He showed the plates to no one until Moroni instructed him to do so.

That was only a slight variation on the first principle Joseph learned—that one does not speak too openly about sacred things.

Joseph Receives the Plates

Shortly after midnight on September 22, 1827, Joseph and Emma Smith left his parents' farm and rode together to the foot of the Hill Cumorah. Emma waited in the carriage while Joseph climbed the hill alone.[71] When Joseph neared the top, Moroni met him and entrusted the golden manuscript of the Book of Mormon to his keeping. As Joseph accepted the plates, Moroni cautioned him again. A paraphrase of that caution, deliciously spiced by the accent and idioms of his mother's own rural New England culture, is given in Lucy Mack Smith's History:

> Now you have got the Record into your own hands, and you are but a man, therefore you will have to be watchful and faithful to your trust, or you will be overpowered by wicked men; for they will lay every plan and scheme that is possible to get it away from you, and if you do not take heed continually, they will succeed. While it was in my hands, I could keep it, and no man had power to take it away! But now I give it up to you. Beware, and look well to your ways, and you shall have power to retain it, until the time for it to be translated.[72]

Joseph recorded a promise from Moroni: "If I would use all my endeavors to preserve them, until he, the messenger, should call for them, they should be protected."[73] Joseph knew he would receive whatever help he needed.

Joseph took the plates and carried them down the hill until he came to a large birch tree, dead and fallen to the ground. He carefully cut the bark of the tree, turned it back, and made a hole in the decayed wood. After hiding the plates inside, he replaced the bark and camouflaged his activity by covering that part of the log with whatever lay nearby. Then, without the plates, he returned to the carriage where Emma was waiting. It was early morning before they arrived at the Smith home again.[74]

Joseph's mother had not been able to sleep that night. Before she went to bed, Joseph and Emma had already left the house together, and Mother Smith knew where they were going. Years later, when she wrote her *History* and recorded these events, she vividly recalled her anxiety. For three successive years she had watched Joseph's disappointment in not obtaining the plates, and she felt she could not bear to see him disappointed again. She "spent the night in prayer and supplication to God."[75]

Joseph and Emma were gone longer than she expected. When they did return his mother saw that Joseph did not have the plates, and her anxiety got the better of her. She "trembled so with fear" that he might have been disappointed again that she felt compelled to leave the room so he would not notice how upset she was. But he did notice. He followed her into the kitchen and said, "Do not be uneasy, mother, all is right—see here, I have got a key." He then handed her the Urim and Thummim. She recounted, "I knew not what he meant, but took the article of which he spoke in my hands and examined it. He took it again and left me, but said nothing respecting the Record."[76]

The Urim and Thummim were Joseph's communications system with the heavens. His mother records that he kept it always about his person.[77] He used it, not only as a learning tool, but also as a kind of alarm apparatus. With its help he "could ascertain, at any time, the approach of danger, either to himself or to the Record."[78]

Joseph's not-so-friendly neighbors were very aware that he had been trying to get this golden book. Hunting buried treasure was a popular pastime in New England in the early 1800s, and some of his neighbors were determined to get a share of the treasure as soon as Joseph found it. It is not surprising that Moroni was concerned and that Joseph had learned to be very cautious.

As soon as he was able, he removed the plates from the hollowed-out log and locked them in a box that he buried under a loose stone in front of the fireplace.[79] However, that hiding place was not secure for long. Joseph's enemies attached themselves to a Miss Chase, who had a "green glass through which...she could discover the precise place" where the plates where hidden.[80] Several times Joseph moved the plates just before she and her followers arrived to search, but each of those times, only the previous hiding place was discovered and the plates remained safe.[81]

Joseph and Emma Move to Harmony, Pennsylvania

While he was under the constant pressure of trying to keep the plates from being stolen, it was impossible for Joseph to bring them out long enough to work on their translation. Consequently, he and Emma decided they would take the plates and move to Harmony, Pennsylvania, where Emma's parents lived.

That decision created a new problem for the Prophet. Those same people who were trying to steal them from his home would probably stop him and search his wagon. He had to find a way of transporting the plates on the wagon without making them vulnerable during such a search. He and Emma were taking a barrel of beans with them to Pennsylvania, and Joseph created a secret compartment by making a false bottom in the bean barrel. He hid the plates in the space between the two bottoms of the barrel and then filled the rest of the barrel with beans.

His precautions were justified. They had gone only a short distance when a determined band of ruffians caught them and searched the wagon. After what must have seemed to Joseph and Emma to be a very long time, the men left without discovering the secret compartment. The plates remained safe,[82] but that does not suggest they overlooked the bean barrel. The simplest way to search it, without emptying out all the beans, would have been to move a sword blade back and forth through the beans to feel if the sword struck anything hard. If that was the way they examined the barrel, the would-be thieves did not notice that the distance from the top to the bottom of the barrel was shorter on the inside than the distance from the top to the bottom on the outside. They assumed the barrel contained only beans.

When Joseph and Emma arrived at Emma's parent's home, Joseph removed the plates from the bottom of the barrel and took them into the house. Later, after they were settled into their own home, Joseph kept the plates wrapped in a muslin cloth, sitting on the bureau. Emma frequently moved them to dust, but she never removed the cloth to see the plates—a fact which says a great deal about Emma's personality, and integrity—and which in turn says a great deal about why Joseph loved her and why she had been chosen to be his wife.

FIFTH PRINCIPLE: FRIENDSHIPS, HOWEVER IMPORTANT, ARE NOT AS IMPORTANT AS KEEPING GOD'S COMMANDMENTS

JOSEPH BEGINS TO TRANSLATE THE PLATES

Joseph never explained how he translated the Book of Mormon except that he did it "by the gift and power of God" and that he had the assistance of the Urim and Thummim; neither did he explain why he could not translate without a scribe.[83] One key to his method may be found in a statement in a revelation that the Lord directed to Oliver Cowdery after Oliver tried, and failed, to translate.

> 7. Behold, you have not understood; you have supposed that I would give it unto you, when you took no thought save it was to ask me.
>
> 8. But, behold, I say unto you, that you must study it out in your mind; then you must ask me if it be right, and if it is right I will cause that your bosom shall burn within you; therefore, you shall feel that it is right.
>
> 9. But if it be not right you shall have no such feelings, but you shall have a stupor of thought that shall cause you to forget the thing which is wrong; therefore,

> you cannot write that which is sacred save it be given you from me.
>
> 10. Now, if you had known this you could have translated; nevertheless, it is not expedient that you should translate now. (D&C 9:7-10).

From this statement one might conclude that after Moroni taught Joseph how to read the "Reformed Egyptian," Joseph needed to go through the same kind of thought process as would any other careful translator. However Joseph did it, it is apparent that it would have been a distraction to him if he had also needed to write as he worked. For at least that reason, Joseph needed a scribe.

There is another, perhaps more important, reason for Joseph to have had someone to help him. If Joseph had simply closeted himself for a while and then come out with the completed translation of the Book of Mormon, there would have been no evidence, except his own word, that he was the translator rather than the author of the book. But since he had several scribes and they all knew that the portion of the Book of Mormon that they wrote was its first and only draft, their work stands as a testimony—not only that Joseph actually did translate the Book of Mormon but also that he did so in an incredibly short time.

At first Emma tried to write for her husband,[84] but household duties prevented her from being a consistent help. Joseph needed someone who could work with him full time.

The most likely person was Martin Harris. He had been Joseph's friend for many years and was the first, outside the Prophet's family, to know about Moroni. Martin had frequently offered to assist his young friend, and now Joseph was ready to accept his help.[85]

But Martin Harris had a domineering wife who had no confidence in her husband. She believed him to be ripe for swindling—too credulous to be able to sort a hoax from the truth. But she was also determined that if there were anything to this gold-plate business, it would be she, rather than her husband, who would profit from it. She would not let the opportunity to acquire some of Joseph's treasure pass her by.

TROUBLE WITH LUCY HARRIS

Mrs. Harris is an important part of the story of the relationship between Joseph and the angel Moroni for three reasons. First, she was the cause of much of the friction between the Prophet and the angel. Second, her being an obstacle to Joseph's work contributed to a number of important events relating to the translation of the Book of Mormon. And third, because she created such trauma for Joseph and for his family and friends (and perhaps for Moroni too, if angels can experience trauma), it is instructive to see how Joseph and the angel dealt with her.

At the time when Joseph and Emma were getting ready to move to Pennsylvania, Joseph owed debts totaling about $50. He did not have the money but did not want the people he owed to think he was leaving town to avoid paying them. He decided he would try to borrow that amount from a friend and then use it to pay everyone else. With this in mind, Joseph asked his mother to ask Martin if he would lend him the money.

When Mother Smith arrived at the Harris farm, she asked Mrs. Harris if she could talk with Mr. Harris. Mrs. Harris wanted to know all the reasons for the visit, so Lucy Smith told Lucy Harris why she had come. To Mother Smith's surprise, Lucy Harris declared that she would give Joseph the money. When Joseph's mother declined the offer, Mrs. Harris announced, "I am coming to your place to see him, too, and I will be there on Tuesday afternoon, and will stop over night."

When Tuesday came, so did Mrs. Harris. Joseph's mother told the story of her visit in some detail, and in doing so, made no attempt to disguise her disdain for the visitor. Mother Smith recounted that after Mrs. Harris was "well seated," she began to quiz Joseph about the plates. She said if he was telling the truth about having them, he must show them to her; then, she said, "she was determined to help him publish them."

He explained he could not show them to anyone. Relative to her offer of assistance, he told her he would prefer to deal with her husband.

That was not the response Mrs. Harris wanted, for, as Mother Smith observed, "she considered herself altogether superior to her husband," and she continued to tease Joseph about seeing the plates.

> "Now, Joseph, are you not telling me a lie? Can you look full in my eye and say before God that you have in reality found a record, as you pretend?"
>
> To this Joseph replied, rather indifferently, "Why, yes, Mrs. Harris, I would as soon look you in the face and say so as not, if that will be any gratification to you."
>
> Then said she, "Joseph, I will tell you what I will do, if I can get a witness that you speak the truth, I will believe all you say about the matter and I shall want to do something about the translation—I mean to help you any way."[86]

With this statement about her wanting a "witness" the conversation ended for the evening.

The next morning, Mrs. Harris reported she had received her witness. She said she had a dream in which "a personage appeared to her" and told her that her attitude toward Joseph and her insistence upon seeing the plates were "not right in the sight of God." The personage then showed her the plates of the Book of Mormon and said to her, "Behold, here are the plates, look upon them and believe." The dream was so vivid to her that she was able to describe the plates "very minutely" to the Smiths.[87]

The dream had satisfied Mrs. Harris's curiosity but not her determination to control this young man and his gold. She did not trouble Joseph about seeing the plates any more that day, but in all other respects she acted just as she had the night before. She would invest in Joseph's treasure whether Joseph wanted a partner or not. He finally gave in, but recognizing that she was not as willing to be useful as she was determined to dominate, he refused to accept her money as a gift. He would not be indebted to her in any way that could not be readily defined and entirely repaid. He agreed to accept $28 from her—but only as a loan.

Joseph realized that if he was to remain free to obey God he could not accept constraining help from anyone. He understood, though Mrs. Harris did not, that one may assist a prophet only if one does not use that assistance as a lever with which to try to control the prophet.

A short time later, Martin Harris insisted on giving $50 to Joseph. In contrast to Joseph's determination to not accept help from Mrs. Harris, he accepted the gift from Martin. He understood it to be an expression of love from Martin, and Joseph's willingness to receive it is evidence that he trusted his friend. Joseph promptly used Martin's money to pay his debts, and he returned the $28 to Mrs. Harris. [88]

MARTIN HARRIS AND PROFESSOR CHARLES ANTHON

After Joseph and Emma moved to Pennsylvania, Martin would join them and act as Joseph's scribe, but in the meantime, there was still the question of Martin's wife. He felt he needed concrete evidence to convince her, as well as some of his relatives and neighbors, that Joseph was telling the truth. He believed the best way to do this was to get some "expert," whose word they would accept, to testify to the ancientness of the writing on the plates and the correctness of Joseph's translation of it.

Joseph understood his friend's need and wanted to help. After he had unpacked and settled into his new home in Pennsylvania, he copied some of the engravings, translated them and gave both the copy of the words and the translation to Martin Harris to take to whatever experts he wished.[89]

When Mrs. Harris learned that her husband was going to New York City, she was determined to go with him. But he was equally determined to avoid taking her. He set off early one morning without telling her, stopping at the Smiths' home and took Joseph's older brother Hyrum instead. Lucy Harris was livid.

When Martin and Hyrum arrived in New York City, they went to Columbia College and saw a Professor Charles Anthon. Anthon taught classical languages, but he did not know Egyptian. Indeed, at that time, ancient Egyptian was an unknown language, and no scholar in the world could read it.[90] When Martin showed him the words Joseph had copied and Joseph's translation of them, the professor, who could not have had the foggiest notion whether they were translated correctly or not, apparently decided to try to impress this country farmer who had come to see him. Martin reported: "Professor Anthon stated that the translation was correct, more so than any he had before seen translated from the Egyptian." The professor also said that the words which Joseph had copied from the plates were authentic ancient writing and that they included Egyptian, Chaldaic, Assyric, and Arabic characters. Martin asked him

Professor Anthon ripped it into pieces

for a written certificate saying that they were authentic so he could show it to his wife and neighbors. The professor wrote the certificate, gave it to him, and then asked how Joseph had found the plates. When Martin told him about Moroni, Anthon decided to have nothing to do with such a thing.

"Let me see that certificate," he insisted.

Martin took it out of his pocket and handed it to him. Professor Anthon ripped it into pieces while he told the farmer that "there was no such thing now as ministering of angels." He said if Martin would bring the golden plates to him, he would translate them. Martin explained he could not and that part of the plates were sealed, to which the professor replied, just as Isaiah had said he would, "I cannot read a sealed book." When Martin left to return home, he did not have the written proof he wanted to show his wife and friends. But he had heard what this and another professor had said, and he had held the certificate in his hands. He now believed more strongly than ever that Joseph Smith's story was the truth.[91]

After Martin returned home, his wife secretly obtained a copy of the papers he had shown to Professor Anthon. Then, as her husband began to make preparations to rejoin Joseph in Pennsylvania, she announced she was going with him. He could bring her home again after a short visit. He was delighted with her apparent change of heart and agreed that she could go. Little did he suspect what else she had planned.

More Trouble from Mrs. Harris

The first night along their journey, they stopped at a public house for supper and bed. Martin, who was unable to contain his enthusiasm for Joseph's work, showed his manuscripts to everyone at the table and began to tell his story. Then, to his utter amazement, his wife upstaged him by producing similar documents of her own. Announcing that Joseph was not the only one who had such a treasure, she put her copy of Joseph's work on display also. She said she could translate as well as he could. She continued to do this at every stop they made, until they arrived at Joseph's home.[92]

As soon as the horses stopped in front of Joseph's house, Mrs. Harris informed her host that she had come to see the plates and would not leave until she had examined them. Accordingly, without delay or permission, she went straight into the house and ransacked every drawer and searched every nook and corner—she went through everything. Joseph got to the plates before she did, took them outside, and buried them in a snowbank behind the house.

But Mrs. Harris was not one to give up easily. After she had searched the house, she went to the backyard. There she found Joseph's footprints leading to the place where the snow had recently been disturbed. She stooped down and began to excavate. Suddenly, as her hand moved through the snow and leaves, a big black snake stuck its face into hers. Its coiling, hissing maneuvers frightened her so that she abandoned her search and ran back into the house.

its coiling, hissing maneuvers frightened

As she warmed herself by the stove, she asked Emma if there were any snakes in that country in the wintertime. Emma told her there were not, of course, because snakes hibernate in the winter. Well, Mrs. Harris had seen a snake and it had given her a terrible fright. She would not go poking about that snow again.

After that, Mrs. Harris declared that she did not believe Joseph had the plates after all and that she would not stay and look for them any longer. She left the Prophet's house, luggage in hand, and went to one of his neighbors. There she told a story of Joseph's duplicity and invited herself to stay with the neighbor for a week or so. Using that house as a base of operation, she devoted her energies to becoming a living expose of Joseph Smith and his angel. She called on all the other neighbors, telling everyone that Joseph was a fraud, that he was only pretending to have the plates so he could swindle her husband out of his property. The neighbors saw her frustration and believed something dreadful must have happened to her. She identified the dreadful thing as her husband's credulous acceptance of Joseph and his revelations. After that, Joseph had the same kinds of problems with his new neighbors as he had with his neighbors in Palmyra.[93]

When Mrs. Harris had spent two weeks stirring Joseph's neighborhood, Martin took her home. He left her in Palmyra and returned to Pennsylvania to write while Joseph translated.

As soon as her husband was gone, Mrs. Harris began to agitate her own neighbors again. She went from house to house, fretting that Joseph was trying to swindle her husband out of all their property. To demonstrate and make her fears seem more real, she stripped her house of almost everything in it (furniture, linen, bedding, and whatever else she could move) and took these things to the homes of her neighbors. She said they had to be safely out of the way when Joseph convinced Martin to give them to him. The people who kept Mrs. Harris's things for her were also the Smiths' neighbors. Soon almost everyone in town began to talk about the Smiths as though they were dangerous, cunning criminals.[94]

The Loss of the 116 Pages

When Martin returned to Joseph's home in Pennsylvania, he and the Prophet focused all their attention on translating the Book of Mormon. Joseph took very seriously Moroni's instruction that no one was to see the plates. Therefore, Martin did not actually watch Joseph as he translated. Joseph sat on one side of a curtain, Martin on the other. Joseph would read each sentence slowly and clearly. When he came to a name that he did not think Martin would know, the Prophet spelled it for him. They proceeded in this way until Martin had written 116 pages in longhand.[95]

By then, Martin could no longer contain his enthusiasm for what he was learning from the translated part of the Book of Mormon. He was sure if his wife could read those things, she would believe him and stop causing so much trouble. Martin asked Joseph for permission to take the manuscript home to show her.

Martin had been Joseph's good friend. He had believed Joseph and trusted him when many other people had only tried to be hurtful: he had defended Joseph against bitter attacks on his integrity; he had made a special trip to New York City to prove to his wife and neighbors that Joseph was telling the truth; and he had spent many hours writing for Joseph while the Prophet translated. Now all he wanted in return was one more chance to prove to Joseph's enemies that the young prophet was not a fraud. Surely, he pleaded, Joseph could do that much for his friend.

Joseph would not agree to the request until he had checked with the Lord. So, using the Urim and Thummim, Joseph asked, and the Lord replied emphatically that he must not.[96]

But Martin's enthusiasm was not that easily tamed. He begged Joseph to ask again, and Joseph did so. The answer did not change. Still Martin was not satisfied.

After more teasing, Joseph agreed to ask the Lord again. This time the Lord consented, but only on two conditions: first, that Martin would make some very restrictive promises about what he would do with the manuscript, and second, that Joseph would take full, personal responsibility for whatever happened. Martin agreed that he would "show them only to his brother, Preserved Harris, his own wife, his father and his mother, and a Mrs. Cobb, a sister to his wife." Somehow that promise did not satisfy Joseph. He felt ill at ease about the whole business and required Martin to "bind himself in a covenant to me [Joseph] in a most solemn manner that he would not do otherwise than had been directed. He did so. He bound himself as I required of him, took the writings, and went his way."[97]

Joseph hoped the precious pages would be safe in Martin's hands, but he also understood that the ultimate responsibility for their safety was his own. He had been in a dreadful dilemma. He liked Martin and appreciated his help. He did not want to be the cause of his friend's unhappiness. He sympathized with Martin, understood about Martin's wife, and believed he could trust his friend. But in helping that friend, Joseph had imposed his own wisdom upon the Lord and had not followed the Lord's counsel. Now, after Martin had gone, the echo of his own disobedience and a foreboding of danger gnawed at the young prophet's consciousness. Martin had taken the only copy of the translation. If it were lost, they did not have a replacement.

Joseph's life had other complications that soon diverted his attention. When Emma gave birth to their first child, the baby died and Emma was so ill and depressed that Joseph feared she might die also. Day and night he sat beside her bed, hardly sleeping. By the time Emma had begun to regain her strength, Joseph was very ill.[98]

As soon as she was well enough, Emma asked Joseph if Martin had returned with the 116 pages. He had not. Joseph had been thinking about that too, but he had said nothing to Emma for fear it might upset her. But now that Emma was feeling better, he did not dare ignore that matter any longer. So, at her urging, leaving her in the care of her mother, he

he stopped, climbed upon the rail fence, and perched there

boarded a stagecoach and rode to his parents' home. When he arrived, he was so ill that his family put him to bed before they sent for Martin Harris.

Martin usually came as soon as he heard Joseph was in town, but this time he did not. The Smiths had expected him for breakfast, but they did not see him until almost noon. His eyes fixed upon the ground, he walked slowly along the wagon road that led to their home. When he got to their gate, he stopped, climbed upon the rail fence, and perched there. He drew his hat down over his eyes and just sat. After a long, long time, he slunk down from the fence and moved toward the house.

Joseph's mother recalls in her *History* that breakfast was still waiting and everyone was ready to eat when Martin came in and sat down at the table. He picked up his knife and fork as though he were going to begin eating and then dropped them again.

Hyrum was the first to respond, "Martin," he asked, "why do you not eat; are you sick?"

Martin buried his face in his hands and began to moan, "Oh, I have lost my soul! I have lost my soul!"

Joseph understood. "Martin, have you lost that manuscript? Have you broken your oath, and brought down condemnation upon my head as well as your own?"

"Yes, it is gone, and I know not where."

"Oh, my God!" Joseph clinched his hands together. "All is lost!" He wept. "All is lost! What shall I do? I have sinned—it is I who tempted the wrath of God. I should have been satisfied with the first answer which I received from the Lord; for he told me that it was not safe to let the writing go out of my possession."

He paced the floor and then stopped to ask Martin to go home and look again.

"No," Martin replied, "it is all in vain.... I know it is not there."

Then Joseph remembered Moroni and wept again. "Then must I return with such a tale as this? I dare not do it. And how shall I appear before the Lord? Of what rebuke am I not worthy from the angel of the Most High?"

His mother, more worried about her son than about the angel, tried to comfort him. "I besought him not to mourn so," she later recounted, "for perhaps the Lord would forgive him after a short season of humiliation and repentance," she suggested. But Joseph could not be comforted, for he "understood the consequences of disobedience." All the rest of that day, he paced back and forth, weeping and grieving, until he was exhausted and finally accepted something to eat.[99]

The manuscript was gone, and no member of the Smith family would ever see it again. The next morning, Joseph left to return to Pennsylvania. It seemed that all his hopes had been shattered by his friend's duplicity and his own unwillingness to obey. As Joseph left the house, a dense fog spread over the dreary countryside. "I well remember that day of darkness, both within and without," wrote his mother many years later. "To us, at least, the heavens seemed clothed with darkness, and the earth shrouded with gloom."[100]

What Happened to the 116 Pages?

Martin Harris really did not know what had become of the manuscript. Here is his story essentially the way Mother Smith was able to piece it together:

Soon after Martin had arrived home with the 116-page handwritten manuscript, he showed it to his wife and the other persons named in his agreement. Then, since he had promised he would show it to no one else, he needed a place to keep it secure until he could return it to Joseph. His wife seemed so pleased with what she read that she permitted him to put it in her own bureau drawer, the only drawer in the house with a lock. This was a special favor, for until that time, Mrs. Harris had never allowed her husband to even look into that drawer.

Days later, when his wife was not home, Martin was entertaining a visitor by telling him stories about Joseph's adventures and the manuscript now in his own keeping. When the friend asked to see it, Martin could not resist. He went to his wife's room to get the papers. As he expected, the drawer was locked, but to his surprise, the key was not in its usual place, and he could not find it. His need to prove that he really had the paper was more compelling than his fear of his wife. He forced the lock, damaging the bureau drawer in the process.

After showing the manuscript to his friend, Martin put the 116 pages into the chest of drawers in his own room. It did not have a lock, but at least he could get at it easily whenever he wanted to show the manuscript again; for, once he had broken his promise to Joseph, he seemed to lose all compunction about showing the papers to just about anyone.[101]

Joseph's mother later accused him of showing them to almost everyone around, "except our family." She complained, "We were not allowed to set our eyes upon them."[102]

When Martin received the message that Joseph had come to Palmyra and would like to see him, he went to his bureau drawer to get the manuscript and take it to Joseph. It was gone. His wife claimed to know nothing whatever of its whereabouts. Martin frantically searched the house, even ripping open their feather beds and pillows in his desperate attempts to find it. After that, there was nothing left to do but go to the Smith home and tell Joseph the manuscript was lost.

Martin never did find the 116 pages. Mother Smith registers her belief that Lucy Harris took them, intending to use them to embarrass Martin and Joseph.[103] Whoever took them, to Joseph they were irretrievably lost.

JOSEPH'S FINAL LESSON ABOUT OBEDIENCE

As Joseph returned to Pennsylvania, he experienced a depth of dejection he had never known before. The responsibility for losing the manuscript was his. He had acted as if a prophet's first responsibility were to his friends. He had weighed what he thought was right against what the

Lord had told him, and he had chosen the former. Now he was alone—utterly, terribly alone. The Lord, knowing Martin's weaknesses and understanding Martin's wife, had warned Joseph it was not safe, but Joseph thought he knew better. Now that the precious pages were gone, he had no purpose—only questions without answers. What would happen? Would the Saviour ever trust him again? How could he face Moroni and tell him the pages were gone?

In his desperate aloneness, Joseph prayed. Moroni came, but in this visit the young prophet found more accusation than comfort. Joseph had delivered the manuscript "into the hands of a wicked man" and had assumed unto himself the responsibility for that man's unfaithfulness. Now it would be necessary for Joseph "to suffer the consequences of his indiscretion." He must return the Urim and Thummim to the angel; he could no longer use them to translate the plates or to communicate with the heavens. As Moroni took them from Joseph, he offered some hope: "If you are very humble and penitent, it may be you will receive them again; if so, it will be on the twenty-second of next September."[104]

Not long after that, on a day when Joseph "was walking out a little distance," Moroni joined him and let him use the Urim and Thummim to receive a revelation from the Lord. Now, from the Saviour himself, the subdued young Prophet received a reprimand. In the revelation, the Saviour faulted Joseph for being so eager to please his friend that he did not pay attention to the instructions from his God. The message was unbending and to the point: Even though one might receive "many revelations" and exercise "power to do many mighty works," if he reduces himself to boast "in his own strength, and sets at naught the counsels of God, and follows after the dictates of his own will and carnal desires, he must fall and incur the vengeance of a just God upon him." (D&C 3:4).

The Lord encouraged Joseph by reminding him who he was—the "Joseph" he had ever been.

> 9 Behold, thou art Joseph, and thou wast chosen to do the work of the Lord, but because of transgression, if thou art not aware thou wilt fall.
>
> 10 But remember, God is merciful; therefore, repent of that which thou hast done which is contrary to the commandment which I gave you, and thou art still chosen, and art again called to the work. (D&C 3:9-10).

After Joseph had received this message, Moroni took the Urim and Thummim from him. This time he also took the plates of the Book of Mormon and left Joseph alone. The Lord later described what happened next:

> 1. ...because you delivered up those writings...into the hands of a wicked man, you have lost them;
>
> 2. And you also lost your gift at the same time, and your mind became darkened; (D&C 10:1-2).

Even though Joseph wrote nothing about those next few days,[105] it is apparent that they were exceedingly important, even pivotal to his maturation. This young man was that "Joseph" who was destined to orchestrate the ultimate destruction of Satan's kingdoms in this world, and the devil, knowing that, tried to destroy him.[106]

"And your mind became darkened." Those are the telling words.

There is no emptiness so complete as when the Spirit of the Lord withdraws and one is left utterly alone.

After awhile, the Saviour spoke to Joseph again, as recorded in Section 10 of the Doctrine and Covenants. More than half of that revelation was about Satan and his servants, who "love darkness rather than light." But the Lord assured Joseph that even as Satan had been unsuccessful in his recent attempt to destroy the young prophet, so he would remain incapable of success because the Lord's wisdom and Joseph's integrity were greater than the devil's power:[107]

> 41. Therefore, you shall translate the engravings which are on the plates of Nephi, down even till you come to the reign of king Benjamin, or until you come to that which you have translated, which you have retained;
>
> 42. And behold, you shall publish it as the record of Nephi; and thus I will confound those who have altered my words.
>
> 43. I will not suffer that they shall destroy my work; yea, I will show unto them that my wisdom is greater than the cunning of the devil. (D&C 10:41-43).

During those days of which there is no record, Joseph had passed one of the greatest tests of his life. The Saviour instructed the Prophet:

> Pray always, that you may come off conqueror; yea, that you may conquer Satan, and that you may escape the hands of the servants of Satan that do uphold his work. (D&C 10:5).

The idea of Joseph meeting and conquering Satan evokes an image of some titanic duel of personalities, similar to when Satan demanded, "Worship me," and Moses belligerently responded, "Where is thy glory, that I should worship thee?" (Moses 1:12-25).

In Joseph's story, that may be just what happened, but, as in Moses's story, there has to be much more to it than that. Joseph's experience was probably much like these words from the Book of Mormon:

> They had viewed themselves in their own carnal state, even less than the dust of the earth. And they all cried aloud with one voice, saying: O have mercy, and apply the atoning blood of Christ that we may receive forgiveness of our sins, and our hearts may be purified; for we believe in Jesus Christ, the Son of God, who created heaven and earth, and all things.... (Mosiah 4:2).

For the young prophet to win his struggle against Satan, Joseph had to divest himself of all his masks and baggage, including his desires for whatever pretended glories men or devils might bestow upon him. Having done so, he could see himself as nothing—as beggar, less than the dust, but willing to obey the Lord as dust obeys.[108] In this he discovered he could seek no greater blessing than the privilege to love the

Lord and to love His children. But before the Spirit could teach him how to do that, Joseph had to qualify himself by actually sacrificing all that he is—not as one boldly striding to the temple where he would place himself as the richest of prizes upon the altar, but as one with a broken heart and a contrite spirit.

To be broken hearted does not mean to be forlorn. Anciently, the heart was considered to be the seat not only of one's emotions but also of one's intellect. When the heart is broken, one becomes "nothing" in all the ways by which he might seek to follow "after the dictates of his own will."[109]

One law of the gospel is that "ye shall offer for a sacrifice unto me a broken heart and a contrite spirit. And whoso cometh unto me with a broken heart and a contrite spirit, him will I baptize with fire and with the Holy Ghost." (3 Nephi 9:19-20).

Thus, when Joseph placed his clean but otherwise imperfect self upon the altar, he offered the only sacrifice that could be acceptable to his Saviour—himself. Then he was triumphant—clothed with neither masks nor pretenses —only himself, but not ashamed. He no longer needed to pretend to be anyone except who he was. His triumph was the discovery of his Self. Having made that discovery, he could also redefine his needs—to love the Lord and to serve His children. And the Lord provides sufficient for those needs.

Clothed now with the power of his own integrity, he could no longer be tempted by the artificial glitter of power, fame, self-aggrandizement, excess physical pleasure, or the accumulation of wealth and useless things. Thus, in Satan's great bag of counterfeits, there was nothing at all with which to tempt this Prophet. Joseph had won. There had been no public fanfare—just the quiet, sure sense that one of the greatest struggles of his life was over and that he had found peace.

That bout with Satan was the critical test and ultimate victory of the Prophet Joseph Smith. He, like Moses, had met his enemy face to face and had defeated him.[110] After that, there was no longer any question about Joseph's place in the eternities—but he, like Moses, still had a great deal to do during the time he remained in this world.

SIXTH PRINCIPLE:
THE LORD HAS ALREADY PLANNED FOR HIS CHILDREN'S SUCCESS

JOSEPH IS TOLD TO TRANSLATE THE SMALL PLATES OF NEPHI

In "the beginning," there was a plan established whereby each child of our Father in Heaven would receive just the right challenges and experiences to be able to define one's Self and one's happiness in terms of the Saviour and His atonement. Accommodations were made in that plan to thwart all the maneuvering of Satan and still leave each person free to choose. The Father had known in advance what Satan would do to try to destroy Joseph and His work and had made all necessary preparations to protect Joseph and still give him the chance to choose.

Thus, after Nephi had arrived in America, the Lord instructed him to make a set of small plates and to "engraven many things upon them which are good in my sight, for the profit of thy people." Nephi obeyed. He spent the next ten years[111] composing and polishing a perfectly structured epic poem that not only told a story, but also described the "goodness and the mysteries of God." (1 Nephi 1:1).

Nephi added to that poem (First Nephi) additional inspired writings (Second Nephi) then gave these small plates to Jacob to be added to and preserved.

A thousand years after that, the Lord instructed Mormon to insert Nephi's small plates, intact without abridging them, into the history he was compiling.

Now, almost 2,500 years after Nephi had written it, the Lord explained to the Prophet Joseph the fruition of his plan:

> 38. ...an account of those things that you have written, which have gone out of your hands, is engraven upon the plates of Nephi....
>
> 41. Therefore, you shall translate the engravings which are on the plates of Nephi, down even till you come to the reign of king Benjamin, or until you come to that which you have translated, which you have retained. (Excerpts from D&C 10:38-41).

The Lord then explained that Joseph was not alone in his task. His assignment was the culmination of the work of many other prophets, and his ultimate success would be, in part at least, because of their great faith and love and their desire that the people of the last days receive the blessings of the gospel.

> 46. And, behold, all the remainder of this work does contain all those parts of my gospel which my holy prophets, yea, and also my disciples, desired in their prayers should come forth unto this people.

---

47. And I said unto them, that it should be granted unto them according to their faith in their prayers;
48. Yea, and this was their faith—that my gospel, which I gave unto them that they might preach in their days, might come unto their brethren the Lamanites, and also all that had become Lamanites because of their dissensions.
49. Now, this is not all—their faith in their prayers was that this gospel should be made known also, if it were possible that other nations should possess this land;
50. And thus they did leave a blessing upon this land in their prayers, that whosoever should believe in this gospel in this land might have eternal life;
51. Yea, that it might be free unto all of whatsoever nation, kindred, tongue, or people they may be.
52. And now, behold, according to their faith in their prayers will I bring this part of my gospel to the knowledge of my people. Behold, I do not bring it to destroy that which they have received, but to build it up. (D&C 10:46-52).

The loss of the first 116 pages of the translation of Mormon's abridgment had served two purposes. First, there is possibly more wisdom than we know in the fact that Joseph's first, perhaps stumbling, attempts to translate were not preserved and were not intended to be preserved. Second, it gave Joseph an opportunity to be challenged and thereby demonstrate his integrity, to learn about obedience and sacrifice, and, after he had met the challenge, to find fulfillment and security in God's love for him and in his love for God. The Lord had foreseen Joseph's need to be taught and had arranged that Mormon's abridgement would be used to school the young prophet. With that accomplished, the abridgement could be replaced by Nephi's testimony.[112]

The loss of the 116 pages had been a hurtful experience for Joseph. The Lord withdrew His Spirit, and Joseph tasted the bitterness of hell.[113] Joseph received a revelation calling Martin a "wicked man" and telling him he could no longer participate in the translation. If Martin had believed that Joseph had contrived his story in order to get rich or that Joseph's revelations were a hoax, this would have been the perfect time for him to respond by exposing Joseph to the world. But he did not; instead, he acknowledged his sins and repented.

The Lord had also foreseen Martin Harris's weaknesses, and gave Joseph assurance that he could be forgiven. In time Martin became one of the Three Witnesses, and for the rest of his life, he testified that the Book of Mormon was truly the word of God.[114]

When Moroni returned the plates and the Urim and Thummim to Joseph, he told him that he could begin translating the Book of Mormon whenever he wished. But Martin Harris, who had "sought to destroy" him, could never again act as his scribe.[115] One cannot honestly assist a prophet unless one's purpose is to serve the Lord.

Since Martin could no longer write for Joseph, Emma took up the task, but housework and other things got in the way. At length the Saviour instructed the Prophet to wait, promising to send someone else in due time.[116]

OLIVER COWDERY COMES TO HELP JOSEPH

Oliver Cowdery, who was almost the same age as Joseph Smith, was the new school teacher in Palmyra. He taught all the grades in the one-room schoolhouse and was paid by the parents of the children who attended. But Joseph's parents, who did not have enough money to pay, gave Oliver board and room in lieu of tuition.[117] After the family learned to trust him, they frankly answered Oliver's questions about Joseph and his "golden book." When spring came and school was out, Oliver decided to go to Pennsylvania to meet Joseph for himself.[118]

Ten months had passed since Martin Harris had lost the manuscript. Joseph did not record how he spent that time, but it is not hard to guess. When Joseph began to translate again, his speed and ability were so much improved that after Oliver arrived, Joseph was able to translate the entire Book of Mormon, as we have it, in less than twice the time it had taken him to complete the small part Martin had lost. During those ten months, Joseph had obviously been doing his homework.

Three days before Oliver arrived at Joseph's home, the Prophet, who now felt confident enough to begin the translation work in earnest, prayed to ask the Lord to send him a scribe. The Lord responded that one would come soon. When Oliver Cowdery got there, Joseph knew more about why he had come than Oliver did. They talked late into the night and again the next day. Then, on the third morning, they began working together on the translation of the Book of Mormon.

For Oliver and Joseph, translating was a learning experience and they were discovering ideas they (or at least Oliver) had never encountered before.

THE RESTORATION OF THE AARONIC PRIESTHOOD

New ideas give rise to new questions. Many of the revelations in the Doctrine and Covenants were given in response to Joseph's questions while he was translating or otherwise reading the scriptures. One of the earliest examples of this resulted in the restoration of the Aaronic Priesthood.

Joseph and Oliver had been working together for about a month when they came to a place in the record that discussed the importance of baptism.[119] Neither of them had been baptized, so they went into the woods to pray and ask about baptism. After walking together for a short distance out among the trees, they stopped at the banks of the ambling Susquehanna River. As they prayed they saw an angel descend in "a cloud of light."[120] The angel introduced himself as John the Baptist. He taught them how to baptize, and he ordained them to the Aaronic Priesthood.

Then, as he instructed, Joseph and Oliver baptized each other. This was apparently the first time Oliver had ever seen an angel. Of that experience he left an account that virtually blossoms with nineteenth-century flourishes of

He ordained them
to the Aaronic Priesthood

language.[121] It is delightful to read, but its contrast with the simplicity of the way Joseph told the story leaves one to muse, "How grateful one is that Oliver was Joseph's scribe instead of the other way around."

The Prophet's version of this experience is, as is his account of the First Vision, expressed in "plain, matter-of-fact, truthful...well-mannered prose."[122]

> Immediately on our coming up out of the water after we had been baptized, we experienced great and glorious blessings from our Heavenly Father. No sooner had I baptized Oliver Cowdery, than the Holy Ghost fell upon him, and he stood up and prophesied many things which should shortly come to pass. And again, so soon as I had been baptized by him, I also had the spirit of prophecy, when standing up, I prophesied concerning the rise of this Church, and many other things connected with the Church, and this generation of the children of men. We were filled with the Holy Ghost, and rejoiced in the God of our salvation.[123]

After they were baptized and the Holy Ghost came upon them, the work of their translation took on an entirely new dimension.

> Our minds being now enlightened, we began to have the Scriptures laid open to our understanding, and the true meaning and intention of their more mysterious passages revealed unto us in a manner which we never could attain to previously, nor ever before had thought of. [124]

That statement by the Prophet should be carefully considered. It tells one a great deal about the translation process and about the value of the Holy Ghost. Notwithstanding all he had seen and heard from the angels and from the Saviour, Joseph did not clearly understand what the Book of Mormon prophets had written about the mysteries of the gospel until after he was baptized. He reported, "We were filled with the Holy Ghost, and rejoiced in the God of our salvation."[125] His understanding of the fullness of the gospel came in the appropriate sequence, after obedience and sacrifice.

The Whitmers Prepare to Receive Their Guests

About a week after the visit of John the Baptist, again while translating the Book of Mormon, Joseph received a warning through the Urim and Thummim. There was a plot brewing to kill him. He and Oliver were to get away from there as quickly as possible. They would be safe, the message continued, if they went to the home of David Whitmer, a friend of Oliver's whom Joseph had never met. Oliver was instructed to write David immediately and invite himself and Joseph to live with the Whitmers while they finished translating the Book of Mormon.[126] Oliver wrote the letter, asking David to bring a wagon to Harmony as soon as he could and to take Joseph and Oliver home with him.

When David received the letter, he asked his parents if Joseph and Oliver could come. His parents did not object, but they were not prepared to receive these unexpected guests. David's father reminded him that there was still much work to be done in the fields, and until it was finished they could spare neither the wagon and horses nor the time to go fetch the visitors. David could go, but not until he had taken care of things at home. The Whitmers did not feel the same sense of urgency the Lord had conveyed to the Prophet—but they would.

The first task was to plow a twenty-acre field. The morning after he had received Oliver's letter, David went out early to get started plowing, but he found someone had taken the plow from the place in the yard where the Whitmer's always kept it. David was amazed when he located it in the field he had planned to plow. During the night someone had used it to plow almost a third of that field, and he hadn't the foggiest notion who might have done it. The plow was left standing in the furrow, as he would have left it. All David had to do that morning was hitch the horses to the plow and finish the job. [127]

The Whitmer's had been sowing wheat just before Oliver's letter arrived. If the seeds were left on the top of the ground they would sprout and die because they could not take root. The wheat had to be harrowed into the earth and that had to be done before David left. There was about as much wheat sown as David could harrow in two days' hard work. There were also several piles of plaster of paris that were to be spread on another field. Plaster of paris was used as a kind of fertilizer and, in its powder form, was sown on a field in much the same way wheat was sown. That job also had to be done immediately, because if the piles of powdered plaster were rained on, they would set up like concrete.

When David went out to harrow the wheat, he had the strong impression that rather than dividing the field into small sections and doing them one at a time, as he usually did, he should drive around the entire field. When he stopped for lunch, he looked around and discovered, to his surprise, that he had harrowed in half the wheat. After lunch he went on as before, and by evening he had finished the entire field. He had done two days work in a single day.

His father was beginning to feel there was something rather pressing about getting Joseph and Oliver. The speed with which the obstacles to David's going were being removed confirmed his feelings. Observing to the family that there must be an "over ruling hand" in this, his father urged David to go get their guests as soon as the plaster was sown.[128] David planned to begin that task the next morning.

As day broke he took a wooden scoop under his arm and went out to sow the plaster of paris. He had last seen it in piles near his sister's home, but when he got to where it was supposed to be, it was gone. He ran to the house and asked his sister if she knew what had happened to it.

She did, and she could not understand why he was upset. The day before, she had watched three men. They had spread plaster faster than anyone she had ever seen before. Even her children had been fascinated by the quickness with

his horses did not tire

which the men moved. They were strangers to her—they certainly did not live nearby—but she supposed David must have hired them.[129]

David and his family were now convinced that something very important was going on and that God intended they should be a part of it. He wanted them to get Joseph and Oliver—and He wanted them to do it now. David hitched up the wagon and started off.

He traveled the 135 miles in a surprisingly short time. As would any good horseman, he kept alert to the needs of his animals. He was in a hurry but knew better than to push them too fast. In the long haul, fatigued horses move more slowly than rested ones. To his amazement, in spite of the distance and their speed, his horses did not tire.[130]

Joseph knew David was coming. He told Oliver when David started from home, where he stopped the first night, how he read the sign at the public house, and where he stopped the second night. When David was only a few miles from Joseph's home, the Prophet knew that too, so he and Oliver walked down the road to meet him.[131]

David was surprised to receive this reception and even more surprised to learn that Joseph had known just when he would arrive. But when Oliver told him how Joseph had described his journey, David became quite convinced that Joseph was a prophet and became more eager than ever to help.

They left for the Whitmer farm almost immediately. Emma stayed behind to look after things, but she would join them a short time later.[132]

Moroni Carries the Plates for Joseph

Joseph did not take the Book of Mormon plates with him to the Whitmers' home because he feared that if he were stopped this time, the plates would be stolen. Instead he gave them to Moroni to carry. The angel would return them to him after the travelers arrived at their destination.

During the trip back to David's home, when David and Oliver were riding on the old-fashioned spring seat in the front of the wagon and Joseph was behind them in the wagon box, a rather extraordinary thing happened. Years later, David recalled that they were driving through "a clear open place" when "a very pleasant, nice-looking old man suddenly appeared" beside the wagon.

"Good morning, it is very warm," the man said as he wiped his forehead with his hand. Oliver and David looked at Joseph, he nodded, and they asked the old fellow to ride with them. He replied, "No, I am going to Cumorah." That name caught their attention. They gazed at him and then for a moment at each other. As they "looked around inquiringly of Joseph, the old man instantly disappeared." David remembered him as being "about five feet eight or nine inches tall and heavy set...; his hair and beard were white... he had on his back a sort of knapsack with something in, shaped like a book." David understood (or was told by Joseph; he does not say which) that this man "was the messenger who had the plates, who had taken them from Joseph just prior to our starting from Harmony."[133]

After the travelers reached their destination and were settled at the Whitmer farm, Joseph went alone out into the garden. There, according to prior arrangements, the Prophet met the angel, who returned the plates to him.[134] The next day, Joseph and Oliver began translating again. In the security of the Whitmer home, they would be able to continue their work without much interference until the translation was completed.

Seventh Principle: The Lord Provides Whatever Help He Understands We Need

Mary Whitmer Sees Moroni and the Plates

While Joseph and Oliver were house guests, the men of the family liked having them around and were glad to help whenever they could. The visitors had little effect on the routine of their farm work, but for David's mother, Mary Whitmer, that was not the case at all. In addition to her usual chores, like gathering the eggs, feeding the chickens, and milking the cows, she now had to fix extra for meals, bake more bread, and wash all her guests' clothes—by hand on a scrub board. It made a great deal of difference to her that there were two more grown men living in her home.[135]

Joseph had kept his promise to Moroni and had not shown the plates to anyone, so Mary didn't know he really had them. It may have seemed unfair to Mary that she should have the burden of looking after these two self-invited guests. She may have complained; if she didn't, she probably wanted to.

One day, Mary went out into the barn. She was startled when she first saw an angel standing there with a knapsack over his shoulder, but his kindly appearance soon caused all her fear to go away. Her description of him was like the description of the old gentleman Joseph, Oliver, and her son David had talked with when they were riding in the wagon.

He said to her, "You have been very faithful and diligent in your labors, but you are tired because of the increase in your toil; it is proper, therefore, that you should receive a witness that your faith may be strengthened." He then untied his knapsack and showed her the golden plates. The angel "turned the leaves of the book of plates over, leaf after leaf, and also showed her the engravings upon them; after which he told her to be patient and faithful in bearing her burden a little longer."[136]

After Mary examined the plates, the angel left the barn. She followed him because she wanted to ask him a question, but he was gone—and he had left no tracks in the newly fallen snow.

The angel's showing Mary the plates teaches about how the Lord looks after His children. The Three Witnesses and the Eight Witnesses saw the plates and they were given the responsibility of testifying that they had seen them and they were told never to deny that testimony. But Mary was not given that responsibility. She was shown the plates because the Lord wished to give her peace and to help her understand.

THE TESTIMONY OF SARAH CONRAD

Mary Whitmer never wavered in her support for Joseph Smith after she saw the angel and the plates. But she did do something to lighten her burden and make it easier to care for her family and guests.

The angel had suggested that she hire someone to help her, so she hired her niece, a girl named Sarah Conrad,[137] to live at the house and help with the chores. She did not tell Sarah what Joseph and Oliver were doing, but it did not take long for Sarah to discover that something unusual was going on. Sarah noticed that the Prophet and his friend "would go up into the attic, and they would stay all day. When they came down, they looked more like heavenly beings than they did just ordinary men."[138]

At first Sarah was curious, but in time their luminous appearance actually frightened her. She told her aunt how she felt and asked what made those men "so exceedingly white."[139]

When Mrs. Whitmer explained to Sarah about the Book of Mormon, she "told her what the men were doing in the room above and that the power of God was so great in the room that they could hardly endure it. At times angels were in the room in their glory which nearly consumed them."[140] The light that shone from Joseph and Oliver's faces came from their having been with the angels.

This explanation was reasonable enough and satisfied Sarah. She not only stayed with the Whitmers, but she also became one of Joseph's good friends. She was baptized, and much later, after she and the other Saints were driven from Nauvoo, she settled with them in Provo, Utah.[141]

Joseph never told his readers how he translated the Book of Mormon except to say that he used the Urim and

Thummim and that he did it "by the gift and power of God." But there are some interesting indications that he had help from other angels besides Moroni.[142]

Sarah's is the earliest of a number of accounts that testify that at times, when the Prophet was receiving revelation or was in the presence of heavenly beings, he, like Moses, actually glowed.[143] Wilford Woodruff tried to describe the Prophet's appearance on one of those occasions. He said, "His face was clear as amber."[144] Philo Dibble, who was present when the Prophet received the revelation that is now the 76th section of the Doctrine and Covenants, reported, "Joseph wore black clothes, but at this time seemed to be dressed in an element of glorious white."[145]

Sarah's testimony that the men who were working on the translation of the Book of Mormon "looked so exceedingly white," combined with Mrs. Whitmer's explanation that "angels were in the room in their glory which nearly consumed them," gives a valuable key to understanding the Book of Mormon and to knowing how it was translated. One may assume that if there were angels in the room, they had some purpose for being there other than just to pass the time of day. Their presence in the translating room certainly had an impact upon the ultimate outcome of Joseph's work.

Angels Help Joseph Translate

Neither Joseph Smith, nor Oliver Cowdery, nor the Whitmers, nor Sarah Conrad left any record identifying who the angels were, but others also knew, and they have given some important information about who the angels might have been.

Elder Parley P. Pratt did not identify the angels by name, but he testified that through Joseph Smith "and the ministration of holy angels to him, that book came forth to the world."[146] His brother Orson added that during those years, Joseph "was often ministered to by the angels of God, and received instruction" from them.[147]

President John Taylor, who was a dear friend and confidant of the Prophet Joseph mentioned some of the angels by name. He said:

> Again who more likely than Mormon and Nephi, and some of those prophets who had ministered to the people upon this continent, under the influence of the same Gospel, to operate again as its representatives? Who more likely than those who had officiated in the holy Melchisedec priesthood to administer to Joseph Smith and reveal unto him the great principles which were developed? Well, now, do I believe that Joseph Smith saw the several angels alleged to have been seen by him as described, one after another? Yes, I do.[148]

On another occasion, when President Taylor was discussing the restoration of the gospel, he said, "I can tell you what he [Joseph] told me about it." Then he told this story:

> Afterwards the Angel Moroni came to him and revealed to him the Book of Mormon, with the history of which you are generally familiar, and also with the statements that I am now making pertaining to these things. And then came Nephi, one of the ancient prophets, that had lived upon this continent, who had an interest in the welfare of the people that he had lived amongst in those days.[149]

President Taylor was even more explicit in another address to the Saints:

> And when Joseph Smith was raised up as a Prophet of God, Mormon, Moroni, Nephi and others of the ancient Prophets who formerly lived on this Continent, and Peter and John and others who lived on the Asiatic Continent, came to him and communicated to him certain principles pertaining to the Gospel of the Son of God. Why? Because they held the keys of the various dispensations, and conferred them upon him, and he upon us. He was indebted to God; and we are indebted to God and to him for all the intelligence that we have on these subjects.[150]

Similarly, President George Q. Cannon once assured his listeners:

> [The Prophet Joseph] had doubtless, also, visits from Nephi and it may be from Alma and others. He was visited constantly by angels.... Moroni, in the beginning, as you know, to prepare him for his mission, came and ministered and talked to him from time to time, and he

> had vision after vision in order that his mind might be fully saturated with a knowledge of the things of God, and that he might comprehend the great and holy calling that God has bestowed upon him.[151]

Joseph said very little about his meeting with Book of Mormon prophets other than Moroni. However, in the famous letter to John Wentworth, the one in which he wrote the Articles of Faith, the Prophet explained that the Book of Mormon came forth only "after having received many visits from the angels of God unfolding the majesty and glory of the events that should transpire in the last days."[152] The "many visits" could, of course, have all been from Moroni. But Moroni is only one angel and Joseph wrote that he had received "many visits from the angels." That statement by the Prophet, coupled with those of his friends, leads one to conclude that the translation of the Book of Mormon was something of a joint effort between Moroni; Joseph Smith, who used the Urim and Thummim; Nephi (probably more than one Nephi); Alma; Mormon; and other original authors of the Book of Mormon.

One cannot read the Book of Mormon without noticing the Lord's promises to the prophets that their messages would be passed on to people in the last days.[153] It is not surprising, then, that those same prophets who wrote those messages should be present with Joseph while he was translating their own writings. If the original authors did help in the translation of their own parts of the book, that would guarantee that the English version of the Book of Mormon says just exactly what the authors wanted it to say.

If it were that important that the words in the Book of Mormon say precisely what they were intended to say, then it is just as important that when one reads the book, one reads to learn—with real accuracy—what it says.

Many who read newspapers, magazines, or novels, have trained their eyes to fly quickly over the words, hesitating only long enough to harvest the gist of the sentences. This reading habit costs them little in understanding. It efficiently lets them know what the authors mean without troubling the reader with knowing exactly what the author says. But if we bring that habit into play when we read the scriptures, it may prevent us from knowing any but the most superficial of meanings. If we do not take into conscious account the fact that its words were selected with extraordinary care, we may be caught making incorrect assumptions about the Book of Mormon by asking vital questions in the wrong order. If one asks, "What is the meaning of this passage?" before one has asked, "What do the words actually say?" the real meaning may ever evade this casual reader. The reason for that is that if we read too casually and assume a meaning before reading the real intent of the words, we may miss that intent entirely. Here is an example:

Quickly read the closing words of Helaman's letter to Captain Moroni.

> 41. And now, my beloved brother, Moroni, may the Lord our God, who has redeemed us and made us free, keep you continually in his presence; yea, and may he favor this people, even that ye may have success in obtaining the possession of all that which the Lamanites

> have taken from us, which was for our support. And now, behold, I close mine epistle. I am Helaman, the son of Alma. (Alma 58:41).

Now consider the four following scriptures. The first is the story of the Saviour's coming to the brother of Jared:

> 13. And when he had said these words, behold, the Lord showed himself unto him, and said: Because thou knowest these things ye are redeemed [present tense] from the fall; therefore ye are brought [present tense] back into my presence; therefore I show [present tense] myself unto you.
>
> 14. Behold, I am he who was prepared from the foundation of the world to redeem my people. Behold, I am Jesus Christ. I am the Father and the Son. In me shall all mankind have life, and that eternally, even they who shall believe on my name; and they shall become my sons and my daughters. (Ether 3:13-14).

In that scripture the brother of Jared's redemption happened at the same time as he saw the Saviour. In the next example, Lehi is talking to his son Jacob who is redeemed because he had seen the Saviour in the past:

> 1. And now, Jacob, I speak unto you: Thou art my first-born in the days of my tribulation in the wilderness. And behold, in thy childhood thou hast suffered afflictions and much sorrow, because of the rudeness of thy brethren.

---

2. Nevertheless, Jacob, my first-born in the wilderness, thou knowest the greatness of God; and he shall consecrate thine afflictions for thy gain.

3. Wherefore, thy soul shall be blessed, and thou shalt dwell safely with thy brother, Nephi; and thy days shall be spent in the service of thy God. Wherefore, I know that thou art redeemed [present tense], because of the righteousness of thy Redeemer; for thou hast beheld [past tense] that in the fulness of time he cometh to bring salvation unto men.

4. And thou hast beheld [past tense] in thy youth his glory; wherefore, thou art blessed even as they unto whom he shall minister in the flesh; for the Spirit is the same, yesterday, today, and forever. And the way is prepared from the fall of man, and salvation is free. (2 Nephi 2:1-4).

The third example is spoken by Lehi about himself.

But behold, the Lord hath redeemed [past tense] my soul from hell; I have beheld his glory, and I am encircled about eternally in the arms of his love. (2 Nephi 1:15).

The final example is Samuel, the Lamanite, explaining the Saviour's atonement and the last judgement.

15. For behold, he surely must die that salvation may come; yea, it behooveth him and becometh expedient that he dieth, to bring to pass the resurrection of the dead,

that thereby men may be brought into the presence of the Lord.

16. Yea, behold, this death bringeth to pass the resurrection, and redeemeth all mankind from the first death—that spiritual death; for all mankind, by the fall of Adam being cut off from the presence of the Lord, are considered as dead, both as to things temporal and to things spiritual. (Helaman 14:15-16).

So, in the Book of Mormon, a meaning of the word "redeem" is that one has come into the presence of the Saviour. Now, in that context, re-read the last words of Helaman's letter:

41. And now, *my beloved brother*, Moroni, may the Lord our God, who has redeemed [past tense] us [both of them] and made us free [probably not a reference to political freedom].
—may the Lord our God, who has redeemed us and made us free, *keep you continually in his presence*; yea, and may he favor this people, even that ye may have success in obtaining the possession of all that which the Lamanites have taken from us, which was for our support. And now, behold, I close mine epistle. I am Helaman, the son of Alma. (Alma 58:41).

With this second reading, one discovers not only a wonderful new facet of both men's biographies, but also an entirely enhanced sense of the meaning of Helaman's greeting, "my beloved brother, Moroni."

The Saviour struggled with his contemporaries over the problem of their hearing his words, but not their meaning. He asked, “Why do ye not understand my speech? even because ye cannot hear my word.” (John 8:43).

The words in the Book of Mormon can be relied on to convey the correct message if one will read them to discover what they actually say. Then, having first learned what the words say, one can, with the help of the Spirit, also discover what they mean.

THE TESTIMONY OF THE THREE WITNESSES

After Joseph and Oliver moved to the Whitmers’ home, it took only about a month for them to finish the translation. Joseph worked on it almost constantly. Occasionally, when Oliver got tired, one of David’s younger brothers, usually John, took his place at the writing table.

Even though Martin Harris could no longer write for Joseph, he was still interested in the project and sometimes visited his young friend at the Whitmer farm. One of those visits occurred about the time Joseph translated the fifth chapter of Ether, which contains the promise that God would appoint three witnesses to see the plates and testify “of a surety that these things are true.” (Ether 5:2-4; See also 2 Nephi 11:3).

After Joseph read this promise, Martin Harris, Oliver Cowdery, and David Whitmer said they wanted to be those witnesses. In their enthusiasm, they asked—then begged—

Joseph to ask the Lord for permission to show them the plates. Joseph did so and was told that his friends could see them if they had sufficient faith and a great desire to assist in the work of the Lord. In this revelation the Saviour also promised that they might see other things that they had not asked to see. He mentioned the Urim and Thummim, the breastplate, the Liahona, and the sword of Laban. (D&C 17:1). But they could not see them now. They had to wait until the translation was finished.

So Joseph and Oliver went on with their work, Martin returned home, and David continued to attend to his duties on the farm.

On the day when the translation was completed, Joseph and Oliver walked together into the field where David was plowing and told him they were finished.[154] Joseph sent a message to his parents, telling them the good news and inviting them to join him at the Whitmer farm. They, in turn, told Martin Harris; for, as Mrs. Smith observed, they still loved him even though his weaknesses had caused them many troubles.[155] When Martin heard the news, he asked the Smiths if he could go with them, and the next morning they all set out together.

The evening they arrived at the Whitmer farm, they all read together from the completed translation of the Book of Mormon. The next morning they gathered again to continue to read. After "the usual services, namely, reading, singing and praying," Joseph arose from his knees and said to Martin Harris, "You have got to humble yourself before God this day, that you may obtain a forgiveness of your sins. If you do, it is the will of God that you should look upon the plates, in company with Oliver Cowdery and David Whitmer."[156]

A few minutes later those four—Joseph, Martin, Oliver, and David—left the others and walked together into the woods near the house. Joseph did not carry the plates with him. Moroni had them and would show them to the Three Witnesses himself.

Joseph Smith, David Whitmer, and Martin Harris each left detailed accounts of what they saw and heard that morning. They are dissimilar enough to enable one to see the event from their different perspectives, but near enough alike that they confirm each other's testimonies. Joseph Smith's account reads as follows:

> Not many days after the above commandment was given, we four, viz., Martin Harris, David Whitmer, Oliver Cowdery and myself, agreed to retire into the woods, and try to obtain, by fervent and humble prayer, the fulfilment of the promises given in the above revelation—that they should have a view of the plates. We accordingly made choice of a piece of woods convenient to Mr. Whitmer's house, to which we retired, and having knelt down, we began to pray in much faith to Almighty God to bestow upon us a realization of these promises.
>
> According to previous arrangement, I commenced prayer to our Heavenly Father, and was followed by each of the others in succession. We did not at the first trial, however, obtain any answer or manifestation of divine favor in our behalf. We again observed the same order of

prayer, each calling on and praying fervently to God in rotation, but with the same result as before.

Upon this, our second failure, Martin Harris proposed that he should withdraw himself from us, believing, as he expressed himself, that his presence was the cause of our not obtaining what we wished for. He accordingly withdrew from us, and we knelt down again, and had not been many minutes engaged in prayer, when presently we beheld a light above us in the air, of exceeding brightness; and behold, an angel stood before us. In his hands he held the plates which we had been praying for these to have a view of. He turned over the leaves one by one, so that we could see them, and discern the engravings thereon distinctly. He then addressed himself to David Whitmer, and said, "David, blessed is the Lord, and he that keeps His commandments;" when, immediately afterwards, we heard a voice from out of the bright light above us, saying, "These plates have been revealed by the power of God, and they have been translated by the power of God. The translation of them which you have seen is correct, and I command you to bear record of what you now see and hear."

I now left David and Oliver, and went in pursuit of Martin Harris, whom I found at a considerable distance, fervently engaged in prayer. He soon told me, however, that he had not yet prevailed with the Lord, and earnestly requested me to join him in prayer, that he also might realize the same blessings which we had just received. We accordingly joined in prayer, and ultimately obtained our desires, for before we had yet finished, the same vision was opened to our view, at least it was again opened to me, and I once more beheld and heard the

In his hands he held the plates

> same things; whilst at the same moment, Martin Harris cried out, apparently in an ecstasy of joy, "'Tis enough; 'tis enough; mine eyes have beheld; mine eyes have beheld;" and jumping up, he shouted, "Hosanna," blessing God, and otherwise rejoiced exceedingly. [157]

Even though David Whitmer was an old man when he was interviewed by Orson Pratt, he described his experience with vivid memory.

> It was in June, 1829, the latter part of the month, and the Eight Witnesses saw them, I think, the next day or the day after (i.e. one or two days after). Joseph showed them the plates himself, but the angel showed us (the Three Witnesses) the plates, as I suppose to fulfill the words of the book itself. Martin Harris was not with us at this time; he obtained a view of them afterwards (the same day). Joseph, Oliver and myself were together when I saw them. We not only saw the plates of the Book of Mormon, but also the brass plates, the plates of the Book of Ether, the plates containing the records of the wickedness and secret combinations of the people of the world down to the time of their being engraved, and many other plates. The fact is, it was just as though Joseph, Oliver and I were sitting just here on a log, when we were overshadowed by a light. It was not like the light of the sun, nor like that of a fire, but more glorious and beautiful. It extended away round us, I cannot tell how far, but in the midst of this light about as far off as he sits (pointing to John C. Whitmer, sitting a few feet from him), there appeared, as it were, a table with many

> records or plates upon it, besides the plates of the Book of Mormon, also the sword of Laban, the directors (i.e., the ball which Lehi had) and the interpreters. I saw them just as plain as I see this bed (striking the bed beside him with his hand), and I heard the voice of the Lord, as distinctly as I ever heard anything in my life, declaring that the records of the plates of the Book of Mormon were translated by the gift and power of God.
>
> Pratt: Did you see the angel at this time?
>
> Whitmer: "Yes; he stood before us. Our testimony as recorded in the Book of Mormon is strictly and absolutely true, just as it is there written.[158]

Martin Harris was not present when David and Oliver saw Moroni and the plates, but his account, also given in an interview, was essentially the same as David's.

> Brother Harris said that the angel stood on the opposite side of the table on which were the plates, the interpreters, etc., and took the plates in his hand and turned them over. To more fully illustrate this to them, Brother Martin took up a book and turned the leaves over one by one. The angel declared that the Book of Mormon was correctly translated by the power of God and not of man, and that it contained the fullness of the gospel of Jesus Christ to the Nephites, who were a branch of the lost sheep of the House of Israel, and had come from the land of Jerusalem to America. The witnesses were required to bear their testimony of these things, and of this open vision to all people, and he (Harris) testified, not only to those present, but to all the world, that these

> things were true, and before God whom he expected to meet in the day of Judgment he lied not. [159]

After they had seen the plates, Joseph may not have jumped up and shouted for joy as Martin did, but his happiness was no less exquisite. Now there were three men who knew, as surely as Joseph knew, the truthfulness of the Book of Mormon. Joseph's mother gave a feel for what that meant to the young prophet. She recalled,

> When they returned to the house it was between three and four o'clock p.m. Mrs. Whitmer, Mr. Smith and myself, were sitting in a bedroom at the time. On coming in, Joseph threw himself down beside me, and exclaimed, "Father, mother, you do not know how happy I am: the Lord has now caused the plates to be shown to three more besides myself. They have seen an angel, who has testified to them, and they will have to bear witness to the truth of what I have said, for now they know for themselves, that I do not go about to deceive the people, and I feel as if I was relieved of a burden which was almost too heavy for me to bear, and it rejoices my soul, that I am not any longer to be entirely alone in the world." Upon this, Martin Harris came in: he seemed almost overcome with joy, and testified boldly to what he had both seen and heard. And so did David and Oliver, adding that no tongue could express the joy of their hearts, and the greatness of the things which they had both seen and heard.[160]

One can sense Joseph's feeling of relief where his history records that the Three Witnesses were now obliged "to fulfill the commandment which they had received, viz., to bear record of these things."

To formally do this, "they drew up and subscribed" to "The Testimony of Three Witnesses" which is published in every copy of the Book of Mormon.[161]

The Testimony of the Eight Witnesses

The day after the Three Witnesses saw the plates, Joseph's parents and Martin Harris returned to their homes in Palmyra. The Prophet, anxious to make arrangements to have the Book of Mormon published, followed them about a week later. Oliver and all the Whitmer family went with him to Palmyra and were guests at the Smith home.

Not long after they arrived, all the men among the visitors, along with Joseph, his father, and his brothers Samuel and Hyrum, walked to a place in the woods near the Smith home. It was a special place to the family, for they often met there for prayer. After the men had gathered, Joseph left them and went deeper into the woods, where he met Moroni. The angel gave Joseph the plates to carry back to his friends. The twelve men present were Joseph, the Three Witnesses, plus eight others who had not previously seen the plates. Joseph let each one take the golden book into his hands and examine it carefully. They paid especial attention to the delicate writing that had been engraved into the metal pages. They did not see the angel or hear the voice, but they knew the plates were real and that Joseph actually had them.[162] The eight who had not previously seen the plates signed their names to "The Testimony of Eight Witnesses," that is also printed in each copy of the Book of Mormon.

After they had seen the plates, the eleven men returned to the Smith home, but Joseph remained behind to return the plates to Moroni.[163]

The Eight Witnesses were: Christian Whitmer, Hiram Page, Jacob Whitmer, Joseph Smith, sen., Peter Whitmer, jun., Hyrum Smith, John Whitmer, and Samuel H. Smith.

CONCLUSION:
JOSEPH HAD LEARNED TO BE A PROPHET

WHAT HAPPENED TO THE GOLD PLATES?

The sacred record was once again in the angel's custody. Moroni did not return it to the stone box on the Hill Cumorah where Joseph found it. He placed it in a cave with other sacred Nephite records.

Two months before his death in 1877, Brigham Young described that cave. He explained that his purpose for telling this story was "so that they [these facts] will not be forgotten and lost." He wanted Latter-day Saints to know and remember what had happened to the plates of the Book of Mormon. The following paragraph is the account of Joseph's returning the plates to Moroni as Brigham Young reported that Oliver Cowdery told it to him:

> This is an incident in the life of Oliver Cowdery, but he did not take the liberty of telling such things in meeting as I take. I tell these things to you, and I have a motive for doing so. I want to carry them to the ears of my brethren and sisters, and to the children also, that they may grow to an understanding of some things that seem to be entirely hidden from the human family. Oliver Cowdery went with the Prophet Joseph when he deposited these plates. Joseph did not translate all of the

> plates; there was a portion of them sealed, which you can learn from the Book of Doctrine and Covenants. When Joseph got the plates, the angel instructed him to carry them back to the hill Cumorah, which he did. Oliver says that when Joseph and Oliver went there, the hill opened, and they walked into a cave, in which there was a large and spacious room. He says he did not think, at the time, whether they had the light of the sun or artificial light; but that it was just as light as day. They laid the plates on a table; it was a large table that stood in the room. Under this table there was a pile of plates as much as two feet high, and there were altogether in this room more plates than probably many wagon loads; they were piled up in the corners and along the walls. The first time they went there the sword of Laban hung upon the wall; but when they went again it had been taken down and laid upon the table across the gold plates; it was unsheathed, and on it was written these words: "This sword will never be sheathed again until the kingdoms of this world become the kingdom of our God and his Christ." I tell you this as coming not only from Oliver Cowdery, but others who were familiar with it, and who understood it....[164]

Moroni allowed Joseph to keep the Urim and Thummim and the Prophet continued to use it to receive instructions from the Saviour.[165]

JOSEPH HAD LEARNED TO BE A PROPHET

There is no evidence that Moroni visited Joseph Smith again in the years that followed, but neither is there evidence he did not. Together they had succeeded in their mission. The gold plates had been kept safe, their translation had been completed, and they were once again in the secure custody of the angel. The translation itself was ready for publication.

For Joseph, there had been other fruits of their extraordinary friendship. The young prince had learned who he was—which is the same as learning why he is and why he must remain true to the law of his own being. He had learned from Moroni how to obey and how to know what to obey. He had learned the meaning and triumph of sacrifice. Then the Holy Ghost opened to his understanding the true meaning of the mysteries of the fullness of the gospel as recorded in the Book of Mormon. As a result, Joseph now had the power to commit all that he had and all that he was to the establishment and growth of the kingdom of God.

By shepherding Joseph through those experiences, Moroni had succeeded in his mission: Joseph had learned to be a prophet.

Joseph had learned to be a prophet

BIBLIOGRAPHY

Anderson, Richard L., "Circumstantial Confirmation of the First Vision Through Reminiscences," *BYU Studies* (Spring 1969), 9:373-403.

Anderson, Richard L., "The House Where the Church Was Organized," *Improvement Era,* April, 1970.

Budge, E. A. Wallis, *Babylonian Life and History* (London, Religious Tract Society, 1925).

Cannon, George Q., *Life of Joseph Smith the Prophet* (Salt Lake City, The Deseret News, 1907).

Cannon, George Q. "Visit to David Whitmer," in Preston Nibley, *L.D.S. Adventure Stories* (Salt Lake City, 1953), 93-97.

Charles, R. H., *The Apocrypha and Pseudepigrapha of the Old Testament* (Oxford, Clarendon Press, 1913).

Cowdery, Oliver, "Letter VII," *Latter-day Saints' Messenger and Advocate,* vol. 1, 155-59; and "Letter VIII," vol. 2, 195-202.

Cowley, Mathias, *Wilford Woodruff* (Salt Lake City, Deseret News, 1909).

Huntington, Oliver B., "Diary," typescript copy at BYU Library.

Jensen, Andrew, ed., *The Historical Record,* Vols. V to IX (Salt Lake City, Andrew Jensen, 1886-1890).

Jensen, Andrew, *Latter-day Saints Biographical Encyclopedia*, 4 vols. (Salt Lake City, Andrew Jensen Memorial Association, 1901-1936).

Jessee, Dean C., "The Early Accounts of Joseph Smith's First Vision," *BYU Studies*, Spring, 1969, 287-91.

Journal of Discourses, 26 vols. (London: Latter-Day Saints' Book Depot, 1854-86).

King, Arthur Henry, "A Man Who Speaks to Our Time from Eternity," *Ensign*, March, 1989, 12-16.

Kirkham, Francis W., *A New Witness for Christ in America*, 2 vols. (Salt Lake City, Brigham Young University, 1960), vol. 1.

Knight, Joseph, "Manuscript of the Early History of Joseph Smith," in Dean Jessee, "Joseph Knight's Recollection of Early Mormon History," *BYU Studies*, Autumn 1976, 31.

Newell, Pearl Bunnel, "History of Sarah (Sallie) Heller Conrad Bunnel," and "My Grandmother Bunnel" (Typed copies in author's possession).

Smith, Joseph, *History of the Church of Jesus Christ of Latter-day Saints,* 7 vols. (Salt Lake City, Deseret News, 1950).

Smith, Joseph Fielding, *Teachings of the Prophet Joseph Smith* (Salt Lake City, Deseret News Press, 1951).

Smith, Joseph Fielding, "Urim and Thummim," *Improvement Era,* June, 1954, 382-83.

Smith, Joseph Fielding, *The Way to Perfection* (Salt Lake City, Deseret Book, 1963).

Smith, Lucy Mack, *History of Joseph Smith by His Mother* (Salt Lake City, Bookcraft, 1954).

Stevenson, Edward *Reminiscences of Joseph, the Prophet* (Salt Lake City, published by the author, 1893).

Woodruff, Wilford, Conference Report, April, 1898, 89.

ENDNOTES

1. For a sense of what Moroni told Joseph, read the scriptures quoted to him by Moroni in J.S. History 1:36-41. 2 Nephi 3:6-15 and 1 Nephi 20 & 21 are also about Joseph Smith and the restoration of the Gospel.

2. I Corinthians 10:13. Joseph Fielding Smith, *Teachings of the Prophet Joseph Smith*, 149.

3. See for example: D&C 50:40, 78:17-18; 2 Ne. 28:30; Alma 12:9-11.

4. Jensen, *Biographical Encyclopedia*, 1:274; Stevenson, *Reminiscences*, 30.

5. Lucy Smith, *History,* 46.

6. Lucy Smith, *History*, 82.

7. See also: Jessee, "Early Accounts," 287-91.

8. Jessee, "Early Accounts," 295. This is the Wentworth letter in which the Prophet Joseph first wrote the Articles of Faith.

9. Jessee, "Early Accounts," 280-81. Frederick G. Williams, the scribe who wrote this account, wrote "a pillar of fire" then crossed out the word "fire" and replaced it with "light." Punctuation is added to this quote because there is none in the original, spelling has been modernized.

10. Jessee, "Early Accounts," 284. Spelling has been modernized and punctuation added.

11. See endnote #18.

12. Ezekiel 1:4.

13. J.S.-History 1:68.

14. Jessee, "Early Accounts," 295.

15. J.S.-History 1:17.

16. Isaiah 6:1.

17. I Nephi 1:8. "Thought" is an interesting word here. We normally use it to suggest that one is not quite sure what one saw, but that is probably not what it means here."Thought" is the past tense of "to think," and if used that way, it says Lehi's was not a passive experience, but one that received his thoughtful attention. Enoch begins his testimony the same way: "Enoch a righteous man, whose eyes were opened by God, saw the vision of the Holy One in the heavens, which the angels showed me, and from them I heard everything, and from them I understood as I saw." Enoch 1:2. (Charles, *Apocrypha and Pseudepigrapha,* 2:188).

18. Among those visions are the following:
Enoch's, recorded in Moses 7:2-4
7:5-67 are about the call (note v. 63-4).
Abraham's, recorded in Abraham 3:22-28
Chapters 4 and 5 continue the story.
Moses's, recorded in Exodus 3:1-15
3:29 to 4:17 the Lord and Moses discuss the call.
Moses chapter 1
The rest of the book of Moses continues the story (note Moses 4:2-3).
Isaiah's, recorded in Isaiah 6:1-13.
Jeremiah's, recorded in Jeremiah 1:4-6
1:7 through chapter 19 the Lord and Jeremiah discuss the call, then there is a short break and the dialogue continues.
Lehi's, recorded in 1 Nephi 1:3-16, 19. See also 2 Nephi1:15.

Ezekiel's, recorded in Ezekiel 1:3-28, 3:12-14
2:1 to 3:11 the Lord explains the call (note v. 7-10).
Alma's, recorded in Alma 36:11-23
Note v. 14 & 22.
Moroni's, recorded in Ether 12:22, 3
Verses23-37 the Lord and Moroni discuss the call.
The Saviour's, recorded in many places. Some are:
John l:1-5 and Joseph Smith Translation, John 1:1-19, 29-33 (page 807-808 of LDS Bible); D&C 93:1-21; Luke 1:69-75; and Isaiah chapter 61.
John the Baptist's is suggested in Luke 1:76-79, and in John 1:33 ("He that sent me to baptize with water, the same said unto me,...").
Joseph Smith's, recorded in J.S.-History 2:15-20
Also in 1 Nephi 20 & 21.

19. See, for example, "a mission and an ordinance" in D&C 77:14; "anointed" Isaiah 61:1 and D&C 138:42; and perhaps "baptized" in 1 Nephi 20:1. Compare: John 1:33, Ephesians 1:4 & 13 and D&C 93:21-22 with D&C 76:51-56. Joseph Fielding Smith cited Ephesians 1:1-3 to show that there were ordinances in the pre-mortal world, *Way to Perfection*, 50-51.

20. As in Alma 13:1 where it is the Father, himself, who performed the ordinations.

21. Jeremiah 1:9-10.

22. Revelation 10:7-11; D&C 77:14.

23. 1 Nephi 1:11-15.

24. Isaiah 6:6-7. Also as in D&C 77:14, "a mission and an ordinance."

25. Isaiah, 6 (Part of 2 Nephi 16 is significantly different.).

26. J.S.-History 1:20.

27. Jessee, "Early Accounts," 280-81.

28. It is reasonable to assume Moroni had read 2 Nephi 3:15.

29. This is not so great a logic leap as it may appear. The list of persons who were present at the meeting in the spirit world over which the Saviour presided between his death and resurrection (D&C 138:38-56), includes persons who had lived on the earth and died (Adam, Eve, Abraham, Isaiah, *et al.*) as well as persons who had not yet been born into this world (Joseph, Brigham Young, *et al.*). So it is evident that prophets from either side of the veil can associate with each other. After the Saviour's resurrection, the next most important event in the history of mankind was the restoration of the gospel. If associations among the prophets who have, and who have not been born in this world, can happen in heavenly councils (as it did on that one occasion) then it seems to me to be unreasonable to suppose that Joseph and Moroni could not have discussed their mutual assignment before Joseph was born. If that is true, then Moroni would have remembered those conversations, but Joseph could not.

30. J.S.-History 1:41.

31. J.S.-History 1:42.

32. J.S.-History 1:46.

33. Lucy Smith, *History*, 78.

34. Many of the details in the following story come from Lucy Smith, *History*, 78-80.

35. Lucy Smith, *History*, 78-79; J.S.-History 1:48-50.

36. Lucy Smith, *History*, 80; J.S.-History 1:50.

37. J.S.-History 1:29; Cowdery, "Letter VII," *M&A*,. I, 155-59.

38. Cowdery, "Letter VIII," *M&A,* 2:197-99.

39. Joseph Smith, *History of the Church,* 1:15-16.)

40. Joseph Smith, *History of the Church,* 4:537.

41. This is Nephi's description of the sword, rather than Joseph's. (1 Ne. 4:9).

42. Joseph Smith, *History of the Church,* 1:12, 16, and 4:537; Joseph Fielding Smith, "Urim and Thummim," 382-83; Stevenson, *Reminiscences*, 24, 27, 31-3; Lucy Smith, *History*, 111-12; 1 Nephi 4:9.

43. Cowdery, "Letter VIII," *M&A,*, 2:196-99; J.S.-History 1:51-52; 1 Nephi 4:9.

44. Cowdery, "Letter VIII," *M&A,*, 2:198; J.S.-History 1:51-52.

45. Cowdery, "Letter VIII," *M&A,*, 2:198; J.S.-History 1:51-52.

46. J.S.-History 1:51-2; Cowdery, "Letter VIII," *M&A,*, 2:198.

47. Parley P. Pratt, *Key to the Science of Theology/A Voice of Warning* (Salt Lake City: Deseret Book Co., 1965), 101.

48. Cowdery, "Letter VIII," *M&A,* 2:199.

49. Cowdery, "Letter VIII," *M&A,* 2:199.

50. Cowdery, "Letter VIII," *M&A,* 2:199.

51. Being true to one's self, true to the law of one's own being, and pulling one's self into square with eternal truth and one's eternal nature, all seem to be the same thing. See: Moroni 7:15-25; D&C 84:44-47; D&C 93:23-28.

52. Joseph Smith, *History of the Church,* 1:16.

53. Lucy Smith, *History*, 81.

54. William Smith, quoted in Anderson, "Circumstantial Confirmation," 399.

55. Lucy Smith, *History*, 82.

56. Lucy Smith, *History*, 83.

57. Lucy Smith, *History*, 84.

58. Lucy Smith, *History*, 84.

59. Joseph Smith, *History of the Church,* 1:16.

60. There is some confusion about when Alvin died. The *History of the Church* 1:2 reads: "...my brothers, Alvin, (who died November 19th, 1824, in the 17th year of his age.)" However, J.S.-History 1:56 reads: "In the year 1823 my father's family met with a great affliction by the death of my eldest brother, Alvin." The *History of the Church* 1:16-17 reads almost the same, except the date is given as 1824. The footnote on page 16 reads: "A genealogy of the Prophet's family in the Church records gives the date of Alvin's death, November 10, 1825. Lucy Smith's *History of the Prophet* agrees with the text above—1824, November 19." To make matters more complicated, my copy of Lucy Smith's *History*, [Bookcraft, 1954, 86] gives the date as 1823.

The story told by Joseph Knight seems to confirm the 1824 date. If it is correct, the chronology would be this:

Sept. 22, 1823, Joseph first sees the plates.
Sept. 22, 1824, Joseph is told that next time he must bring Alvin.
Nov. 19, 1824, Alvin died.
Sept. 22, 1825, Joseph is told he must choose someone else to bring.
Sept. 22, 1826, Joseph and Emma go to the hill to get the plates.

61. See Mormon 8:1-4.

62. Knight, "Manuscript," 31. Spelling and punctuation have been modernized.

63. Knight, "Manuscript," 31.

64. See D&C 9:7-9.

65. Knight, "Manuscript,"31.

66. Lucy Smith, *History*, 100.

67. Lucy Smith, *History*, 101.

68. Lucy Smith, *History*, 100-01.

69. Cowdery, "Letter VIII," *M&A,* 2:201-02.

70. Ether 5:1-4.

71. Details of this story are found in the Joseph Knight "manuscript," and in Lucy Smith's *History*, 102-04.

72. Lucy Smith, *History*, 110.

73. Joseph Smith, *History of the Church,* 1:18.

74. Lucy Smith, *History*, 102-04.

75. Lucy Smith, *History*, 102.

76. Lucy Smith, *History*, 104.

77. Lucy Smith, *History*, 107.

78. Lucy Smith, *History*, 110.

79. Lucy Smith, *History*, 104-112; Joseph Smith, *History of the Church,* 1:18-19 and 4:538; Jensen, 238-39.

80. Lucy Smith, *History,* 113.

81. Lucy Smith, *History,* 107, 110, 113.

82. Lucy Smith, *History*, 118-19; George Q. Cannon, *Life of Joseph Smith,* 48.

83. D&C 1:24, 25:4, 45:60; Book of Mormon title page; Joseph Smith, *History of the Church,* 1:19, 4:537. *America* (Salt Lake City, 1960), vol. 1, 195-96.

84. Kirkham, *New Witness*, 1:195-96.

85. Lucy Smith, *History*, 114; Joseph Smith, *History of the Church,* 1:19.

86. This story is reported in Lucy Smith, *History*, 114-117.

87. Lucy Smith, *History*, 117.

88. Lucy Smith, *History*, 117-18. Joseph Smith, *History of the Church,* 1:19.

89. Cannon, "Visit to David Whitmer,"93-97; Cannon, *Life of Joseph Smith*, 51; Stevenson, *Reminiscences,* 32-33.

90. At that time no Egyptologist could have given honest verification of Joseph Smith's translation of the plates.

The Rosetta Stone, which became the key to the deciphering of ancient Egyptian hieroglyphics, was discovered in 1799. It contains the same message repeated three times: once in Greek, once in Egyptian demotic (every-day Egyptian of the time of the Roman Empire), and once in Egyptian hieroglyphics. Scholars could read the Greek, so used it as a key to learn to read the other.

The original deciphering was done by an Englishman named Thomas Young. Young wrote the article about hieroglyphics which appeared in the 1824 edition of the *Encyclopaedia Britannica*, but at that time he could do little more than identify some hieroglyphic forms of prominent names (Ptolemy and Cleopatra) and to point out that one reads the hieroglyphic words in the direction the animals and birds are facing.

Young's work was amplified by Jean Champollion, director of the Egyptian museum at the Louvre. In 1824 Champollion published *Precis du systeme hieroglyphique* which was a summary of his preliminary work on hieroglyphic translation. Even though this work is now considered to be very important, it was not well received by classical scholars at the time. Consequently it was not widely circulated.

Champollion died in 1831, the year after the Book of Mormon was published, but his colleagues in France continued his work. His *Egyptian Grammar* (1836-41) and *Egyptian Dictionary* (1842-42) were published posthumously.

Professor Anthon taught Greek at Columbia College. Neither his academic background nor the fact that he was in a relatively obscure American college argue for his knowing anything about Champollion's work. It is very unlikely that Anthon had any better information about the Egyptian language than what he might have found in Young's *Britannica* article.

At the time Martin Harris took the Book of Mormon transcript to Professor Anthon, neither Young nor Champollion could have read Egyptian. They could, no doubt, have been able to recognize whether or not the manuscript was written in Egyptian characters. But Professor Anthon, it seems, was not even able to do that.

91. Joseph Smith, *History of the Church,* 1:19-20; J.S.-History 1:64-5; Isaiah 29. Martin Harris did not learn of this prophecy in Isaiah 29 until after his encounter with Professor Anthon, Stevenson, *Reminiscences*, 31-4. *Millennial Star*, 21:545-46.

92. Lucy Smith, *History*, 120-21.

93. Lucy Smith, *History*, 121-22.

94. Lucy Smith, *History*, 122-23.

95. For an excellent discussion of how Joseph translated the Book of Mormon see: Elder Neal A. Maxwell, "By the Gift and Power of God," *Ensign*, Jan. 1997, 36-40.

96. Joseph Smith, *History of the Church,* 1:20-21.

97. Joseph Smith, *History of the Church,* 1:20-21.

98. Lucy Smith, *History*, 124-25.

99. Lucy Smith, *History*, 128-9.

100. Lucy Smith, *History*, 132.

101. All of the following story is taken from Lucy Smith, *History*, 130-32.

102. Lucy Smith, *History*, 131.

103. Lucy Smith, *History*, 131-32.

104. Lucy Smith, *History*, 134.

105. Joseph reports: "...both the plates and the Urim and Thummim were taken from me again; but in a few days they were returned to me, when I inquired of the Lord, and the Lord said thus unto me [D&C 10 follows]." Joseph Smith, *History of the Church,* 1:23.

106. D&C 10:33. There is an interesting story told in the sacred writings of ancient Babylon and Egypt. It is that the devil knows the foreordination of each individual, and uses that information to destroy the individual and thwart the purposes of God. It is that the power of darkness arms itself with the Tablet of Fate "on which the destiny of every man was written at or before the creation of the world," and using the weapon of this information, "the personification of chaos, night, darkness and inertness, and of every kind of evil... would fight the gods and abolish their arrangement of heaven and earth." (E. A. Wallis Budge, *Babylonian Life and History* [London, Religious Tract Society], 1925, 80.)

107. This is the same story as is told in the book of Job—that is, the central issue is the same. "Dost thou still retain thine integrity?" Job 2:3, 9; 27:5; 31:6.

108. See: Helaman 12:7-8, Mosiah 2:25. Immediately before he describes his own bout with Satan, Moses discovered for himself, "Man is nothing, which thing I never had supposed." Moses 1:10.

109. D&C 3:4. John 5:30, 6:38-40. Alma 42:7. "Our first parents were cut off both temporally and spiritually from the presence of the Lord; and thus we see they became subjects to follow after their own will."

110. Moses, chapter one.

111. 2 Nephi 5:28-34. In verse 28 Nephi says, "And thirty years had passed away from the time we left Jerusalem." He then tells that the Lord instructed him to write First Nephi. Later, he adds, "forty years had passed away." It seems reasonable to suppose those ten years, otherwise unaccounted for, were spent in writing First Nephi and the first few chapters of Second Nephi.

112. D&C 10; See 1 Nephi 9:2-6 and Words of Mormon.

113. D&C 19:20.

114. See statement of David Whitmer in Jensen, *Biographical Encyclopedia*, 1:264.

115. Lucy Smith, *History*, 135.

116. Lucy Smith, *History*, 141.

117. Joseph Smith, *History of the Church,* 1:32.

118. Lucy Smith, *History*, 138-41.

119. There are several such places; Mosiah 18:10, and 3 Nephi 11:21-34 are two of the more striking.

120. J.S.-History 1:68.

121. Published at the end of the Pearl of Great Price, 58-59.

122. King, "A Man Who Speaks," 12-16.

123. Joseph Smith, *History of the Church,* 1:42.

124. Joseph Smith, *History of the Church,* 1:43.

125. Joseph Smith, *History of the Church,* 1:43.

126. Lucy Smith, *History,* 147. See also, statement of David Whitmer in Jensen, *Biographical Encyclopedia*, 1:264.

127. Lucy Smith, *History*, 147.

128. Lucy Smith, *History*, 148.

129. Lucy Smith, *History*, 148-49.

130. Lucy Smith, *History*, 149.

131. Jensen, *Biographical Encyclopedia*, 1:267.

132. Lucy Smith, *History*, 150.

133. Jensen, *Biographical Encyclopedia*, 1:267.

134. Lucy Smith, *History,* 150.

135. Jensen, *Biog. Enc,* 1:267.

136. Jensen, *Biog. Enc,* 1:267.

137. Newell, "History of Sarah (Sallie) Heller Conrad Bunnel," and "My Grandmother Bunnel."

138. Interview statement reported in, Richard L. Anderson, "The House Where the Church Was Organized,"*Improvement Era,* April, 1970, 21.

139. Oliver B. Huntington, "Diary," typescript copy at BYU Library. vol. 2, 415-16. Huntington heard this story from Sarah, herself, when she was 88 years old.

140. Huntington, "Diary," 2:415-16.

141. Huntington, "Diary," 2:415-16. See also Anderson, "The House," *Improvement Era*, April, 1970 21. I have also spoken with Sarah's

descendants who confirmed the story.

142. For an authoritative discussion of how Joseph translated, see: Elder Neal A. Maxwell, "By the Gift and Power of God," *Ensign*, Jan. 1997, 36-40.

143. Exodus 34:29-35.

144. Wilford Woodruff, *Conference Report*, April, 1898, 89.

145. *Juvenile Instructor*, 27:303-04.

146. *Journal of Discourses*, 9:212. See also: *Journal of Discourses*, 3:185.

147. *Journal of Discourses,* 15:185. See similar testimonies in *Journal of Discourses,* 13:66 and 14:140.

148. *Journal of Discourses,* 21:163-64.

149. *Journal of Discourses,* 21:161-62.

150. *Journal of Discourses,* 17:375-76.

151. *Journal of Discourses,* 23:363.

152. Joseph Smith, *History of the Church,* 4:537.

153. For examples see: 2 Nephi 33:3-4; 3 Nephi 5:18; Mormon 8:12, 9:30-31; Enos 1:15-16; Ether 12:25-29. See also, 2 Nephi 3:19-21, 26:16, chapter 27; Mormon 5:12-13; Mosiah 1:7; D&C 17:6, D&C 10:46-53.

154. Cannon in Nibley, *LDS Stories*, 96.

155. Lucy Smith, *History*, 151, and 105 with footnote.

156. Lucy Smith, *History*, 151-52.

157. Joseph Smith, *History of the Church,* 1:54-55.

158. Cannon in Nibley, *LDS Stories*, 96; Jensen, *Biographical Encyclopedia*, 1:266, 270; also D&C 17:1.

159. Jensen, *Biographical Encyclopedia*, 1:275.

160. Lucy Smith, *History*, 152-53.

161. Joseph Smith, *History of the Church,* 1:56-57.

162. Lucy Smith, *History*, 154.

163. Lucy Smith, *History*, 155, Joseph Smith, *History of the Church,* 1:18.

164. Oliver Cowdery described this experience to at least two people: The one quoted is Brigham Young (*Journal of Discourses,* 19:38-39); the other is David Whitmer in Stevenson, *Reminiscences,* 14-15.

165. I am not aware of any sure evidence of what ultimately happened to the Urim and Thummim. Joseph apparently had it for several years after he returned the plates to Moroni. See, Stevenson, *Reminiscences,* 5; *Millennial Star* 3:47. Cowley, *Wilford Woodruff,* 157, says Joseph had it in 1841. There is a notarized statement by William Clayton, printed in Jensen's *Historical Record*, 6:225-26, that also says Joseph had it in Nauvoo. Another statement by Heber C. Kimball in 1853 (*Journal of Discourses,* 2:111) says Brigham Young had it at that time.

INDEX

C

D

E

F

G

H

I

J

K

L

M

N

O

P

R

S

T

U

W

Y

EBORN BOOKS MORMON LIBRARY SERIES

☐ *The Seer*. Orson Pratt

☐ *Joseph Smith As Scientist.* John A. Widtsoe

☐ *Key to the Universe*. Orson Pratt

☐ *Life of David W. Patten, The First Apostolic Martyr*. Lycurgus Wilson

☐ *Life of Joseph the Prophet*. Edward W. Tullidge

☐ *Bruce R. McConkie. Highlights From His Life & Teachings*. Dennis B. Horne

☐ *Counselors to the Prophets.* Michael K. Winder

☐ *Called of God by Prophecy*. Dennis B. Horne

☐ *Presiding Bishops*. Michael K. Winder

☐ *Book of Mormon Summary*. Mark A. Smith

☐ *The Power of God.* Mark A. Smith

☐ *Only Repentance*. Mark A. Smith

☐ *Turn on the Power!* Rulon G. Craven

☐ *Animals and the Church*. Gerald E. Jones

☐ *Joseph & Emma's Julia, The Other Twin*. S. Reed Murdock

☐ 1830 Book of Mormon (Facsimile Reprint)

☐ *The Joseph Smith Family.* Ben Bridgstock

☐ *Determining Doctrine.* Dennis B. Horne

☐ *Murder of the Mormon Prophet.* LeGrand Baker

☐ *Joseph & Moroni. The 7 Principles Moroni Taught Joseph Smith.* LeGrand Baker